Readings in Literary Criticism 14
CRITICS ON T.S. ELIOT

KU-451-697

Readings in Literary Criticism

K

CRITICS ON
T. S. ELIOT

Readings in Literary Criticism

Edited by Sheila Sullivan

London · George Allen and Unwin Ltd

FIRST PUBLISHED IN 1973

This book is copyright under the Berne Convention. All rights are reserved. Apart from any fair dealing for the purpose of private study, research, criticism or review, as permitted under the Copyright Act, 1956, no part of this publication may be reproduced, stored in a retrieval system, or transmitted, in any form or by any means, electronic, electrical, chemical, mechanical, optical, photocopying, recording or otherwise, without the prior permission of the copyright owner. Enquiries should be addressed to the publishers.

© *George Allen & Unwin Ltd 1973*

ISBN 0 04 821032 3

PRINTED IN GREAT BRITAIN
in 10 point Plantin type
BY CLARKE, DOBLE & BRENDON LTD
PLYMOUTH

CONTENTS

INTRODUCTION

Already there is a flourishing industry in Eliot criticism, much of which floats, as Hugh Kenner puts it, in a cloud of unknowing. Almost every conceivable interpretation and every style of criticism, from the charmingly dotty to the impenetrably profound, has somewhere found its way into print. Although bewildering, this variety is a compliment to both author and critics, for it represents a vigorous attempt to answer the challenge set by Eliot's work. With the help of the Introduction and Bibliography, I hope to provide in the body of this book some guide through this sacred wood.

Although in retrospect most critics agree that Eliot's work can be seen as an interrelated and organic growth, his apparent changes of direction have always been disconcerting. Those brave early admirers whose voices sounded through a hubbub of jeers (it is difficult now to imagine the outrage provoked by 'The Waste Land') were brought up sharply by Eliot's announcement in 1928 that he considered himself a classicist, a royalist, and an Anglo-Catholic. A later generation of admirers was equally startled by the apparent contrast between the 'Four Quartets' and the West End plays. Mr Eliot did not help very much, for he never cared for explanations. The Notes to 'The Waste Land' characterize this habit nicely; were they merely, as Mr Eliot asserted, added at the request of his publisher to fill up a few blank sheets? In an extract in this book, George Williamson makes illuminating use of them, but there are other critics who regard them as less than helpful. Then, as ever, Old Possum lay low, choosing neither to make the way clear nor the meaning plain.

For good or ill, the influence of Eliot's poetry has been immeasurable. After 'Prufrock' in 1917, and certainly after 'The Waste Land' in 1922, it was no longer possible for a serious poet to write in the manner of the Georgians. His poetry emerged, even then, assured and mature, exactly matching the manner to the intention, and from the beginning his touch was lethal to the Georgian style. With Pound and Laforgue behind him, he created a revolution.

John Crowe Ransom, Conrad Aitken, Edwin Muir, F. R. Leavis and a few others recognized in the twenties that a new master had appeared, but even when the aged eagle spread his wings in 'Ash Wednesday' in 1930 there were still many who would not acknowledge his majesty. He was a bird of prey only, they said, who snatched what he required from other men's acres and produced nothing readable of his own. Nevertheless, about 1930 was the turning point. From then on, slowly but inexorably, Eliot's reputation grew, the clamour subsided to a respectful murmur, and when he died in 1965 he was regarded by the public as the most eminent and the most respectable man of letters in the English-speaking world.

But among critics the debate is by no means over. For this book I have chosen extracts from writers who are in the main admirers of Eliot, for it seemed they had the most useful and perceptive things to say. But I have included a passage by D. S. Savage, who finds a serious falling off in the later poetry, and I should have liked to have had space to include the strictures and reservations of David Daiches, F. W. Bateson and Donald Davie, whose articles are listed in the Bibliography. Those who prefer a drop more vitriol with their criticism should refer to Yvor Winters's *Anatomy of Nonsense* and R. H. Robbins's 'The T. S. Eliot Myth'.

I have deliberately omitted from this selection three books which are vital to any study of Eliot. But they are readily available almost anywhere, and my omission of them is for that reason only. They are F. O. Matthiesen's *The Achievement of T. S. Eliot*, Helen Gardner's *The Art of T. S. Eliot* and Raymond Preston's *The 'Four Quartets' Rehearsed*; details are in the Bibliography. I regret that I have had no space to include passages on Eliot's literary criticism, or for studies of his writings on culture and society.

It is difficult to tell so soon after a poet's death what will become of his reputation. Eliot's still stands very high, but there are signs of doubt and disaffection creeping in. It may be that the next ten years will see a revaluation, and probably the customary period of neglect will follow later still. But it is hard to see at the moment how Eliot could ever be relegated from his position as one of the two or three most creative and influential figures in twentieth-century literature.

London, 1971   *Sheila Sullivan*

ACKNOWLEDGEMENTS

We are grateful to the following for permission to use copyright material from the works whose titles follow in brackets:

Eyre and Spottiswoode (Publishers) Ltd (Elizabeth Drew's *T. S. Eliot: The Design of His Poetry*; Mrs A. H. Savage (D. S. Savage's *The Personal Principle*); Routledge and Kegan Paul Ltd (D. E. S. Maxwell's *The Poetry of T. S. Eliot*); F. W. Bateson (Keith Wright's 'Word Repetition' from *Essays in Criticism*, Vol. 16, No. 2, 1966); Arizona Quarterly (John B. Vickery's ' "Gerontion": The Nature of Death and Mortality' in *Arizona Quarterly*, Vol. 14, No. 2, 1958); University of Chicago Press (George Williamson's 'The Waste Land' from *Modern Philology*, Vol. 47, No. 1, 1949); University of Natal Press (Audrey F. Cahill's 'The Hollow Men' from *T. S. Eliot and the Human Predicament*); Dennis Dobson Ltd (E. E. Duncan Jones's 'Ash Wednesday' from *T. S. Eliot: A Study of his Writings by Several Hands*, edited by B. Rajan); University of Chicago Press (Grover Smith's *T. S. Eliot's Poetry and Plays*, 1960); Charles Skilton Publishing Group (Frank Wilson's *Six Essays on the Development of T. S. Eliot*, Fortune Press); Bowes and Bowes Ltd (John F. Danby's The 'Four Quartets' from *The Cambridge Journal*, Vol. 4, No. 2, 1948–9); The University of the South (John Peter's 'Murder in the Cathedral' from *The Sewanee Review*, Vol. 61, 1953); Princeton University Press (Carol H. Smith's *T. S. Eliot's Dramatic Theory and Practice: From 'Sweeney Agonistes' to 'The Elder Statesman'*, © 1963 by Princeton University Press, Princeton Paperback 1968); F. W. Bateson (Walter Stein's 'After the Cocktails' from *Essays in Criticism*, Vol. 3, No. 1, 1953); Modern Language Association of America (Robert A. Colby's 'The Confidential Clerk' from *PMLA*, Vol. 72, No. 4, 1957); English Literary Society of Japan (Peter Milward's 'The Elder Statesman and The Waste Land' from *Studies in English Literature*, English number 1967).

ELIZABETH DREW

Belief and Achievement

. . . Integration is central to all Eliot's ideas of life and of poetry. The concept in which both are grounded is that of a pattern of creative order. His review of 'Ulysses' hailed the method of myth as a way of ordering, of giving shape and significance to vision, and when *mythos* and *logos* have become inseparable it is the same. It is the theme behind everything he has written in both poetry and prose. . . .

Eliot sees on the one hand, the world of natural order, with its great organic cycles of birth-death, winter-summer, day-night, and its great harmonious tensions of energy holding all together in pattern. This is the cycle and pattern which Joyce took as his controlling symbol in *Finnegans Wake*. The title suggests that human life is one vast funeral, and yet a matter of rejoicing, since life and death, joy and sorrow, are inextricably one. Moreover the cycle of historical experience, and the river of life, and man himself as the microcosm of both, are all inexhaustible, and their contemplation is sufficient for the human imagination.

But to Eliot such experience and such contemplation are inadequate. Natural law is meaningless, unless complemented and completed by spiritual law, and these two creative 'spheres' become united in the symbol of Incarnation. Capitalized, it is the ultimate symbol of revelation, illumination, transfiguration. But it is also the process at work in all man's true experiences of self-fulfilment. On earth, in religious experience, it has its highest reflection in the symbol of the saint, which Eliot has used in one of his plays. In the secular world its revelation is the presence of art, and that is the symbol which he chose as the title of 'Four Quartets'. On the musical side perhaps we can expand and extend its overtones to include 'the music of the spheres!' But Eliot is a poet and his own creative sphere is that of poetry. The relation of poetry to the central symbol is of a very precise kind. The ultimate revelation is the image of communication by *speech*: the Word. Hence in the world of human communication by speech, poetry is its most perfect counterpart; the revelation and illumination and transfiguration of life through the word.

This cannot be accomplished by the poet without a discipline parallel to that practised in the dedication to the life of religious devotion. It is only by the loss of self in his art that the poet's consciousness is directed, ordered, focused, intensified, and thus made ever more powerful in the diffusion of its energy beyond itself. 'One is prepared for art when one has ceased to be interested in one's own emotions except as material. . . . Personal emotion, personal experience is extended and completed in something impersonal—not in the sense of something divorced from personal experience and passion. No good poetry is the latter. . . . Not our feelings, but the pattern we make of our feelings is the centre of value.'[1] This was written in 1924, but Eliot's theory and practice of poetry have been consistent throughout his life. The things he was actively engaged in battling for when he started writing are the things he continues to battle for, but the feelings and the patterns made of the feelings have steadily changed and deepened.

He has always been master of what, in a rare lapse into the hideous language of modern abstraction, he has called the 'objective correlative'. In 'Prufrock' that creation of thinking into feeling, of projecting the inner life in terms of weather and scenery and rooms and gestures and disease and sounds and textures, seemed already complete. With age he has lost none of that richness of sensibility, but it has been expanded to cover wider areas of experience. And in addition to this he has developed a new method of direct philosophical analysis in poetic form, and has infolded the two into a poetry of contemplation which is as sensuous as it is intellectual. The subject contemplated is pattern; a pattern which, the further it is explored in any direction, up or down, inwards or out-wards, forward or back, is found to be one vast system of dynamic ordered relationships. And so it is with the poetry itself. It has all the qualities alive in the earlier poetry; acuteness of sensibility, structural strength and elasticity, rhythmical variation, absorption of the past and its re-creation into new poetic life. But whereas in the early poems these qualities had often to be asserted through a *dislocation* of language, in 'Four Quartets' they are knit into a perfect articulation of sound and movement and meaning. Instead of dramatic clashes and startling associations and references which require constant elucidation from out-side the poems, the language itself penetrates more and more deeply into the structure, the *word* becomes more and more loaded with meaning. It is squeezed and squeezed of every drop of its juice. It is ex-pression at its fullest.

The 'familiar compound ghost' said of poets:

> our concern was speech, and speech impelled us
> To purify the dialect of the tribe
> And urge the mind to aftersight and foresight . . .

The purification and the replenishment of the English language is a continuous process in Eliot's poetry, and we might extend his descrip-tion of the phrase or sentence that is 'right' very widely.

> (where every word is at home,
> Taking its place to support the others,

[1] T. S. Eliot, Introduction to *Le Serpent* by Paul Valéry.

The word neither diffident nor ostentatious,
An easy commerce of the old and the new,
The common word exact without vulgarity,
The formal word precise but not pedantic,
The complete consort dancing together)

But the ghost added that speech compels the poet 'to urge the mind to aftersight and foresight'. The dialect of the tribe is inextricably inter-woven with the life of its members and with life in general. The life of the word extends beyond itself, not only backwards into the family history of the language, not only around itself in its context, and from there in linked relationships to other parts of the poetic pattern, but to a human context. 'The complete consort dancing together' is not only the organic affinity of the words in the poetic structure, it is also the inter-relationship and inseparability of poetry and life. When the poet is at work, says Eliot, 'he is no more concerned with the social consequences than the scientist in his laboratory—though without the context of use to society, neither the writer nor the scientist could have the conviction which sustains him'.[2]

The poet's own immediate task is to bring all the depth and intensity of his own full consciousness to a verbal surface: the reader, starting from the surface, penetrates gradually to the full consciousness beneath. Poetry is thus both act and instrument. It is the poet's tongue speaking 'a language of enticement' to his fellow men, and urging them, through a sharing of his speech, to share his own aftersight, foresight and insight.

In expressing what other people feel he is also changing the feeling by making it more conscious; he is making people more aware of what they feel already, and therefore teaching them something about themselves. But he is not merely a more conscious person than the others; he is also individually different from other people and from other poets too, and can make his readers share consciously in new feelings which they had not experienced before.[3]

In 'Four Quartets' the poet is trying to awaken the consciousness of his age to its situation. He does not urge the tribe to a religious and political viewpoint by preaching or argument, he urges them to sight through vision.

Nothing could be clearer than the vision of western civilization he creates. We see man, having solved all the problems 'confronting the builder of bridges', living among his metalled roads, his ocean liners, his aerials, his Directory of Directors. He 'tends to forget' the strong brown god, the demonic chthonic powers by which he may be driven, and who use 'the worshippers of the machine' for their own purposes;

---

[2] *The Music of Poetry.*
[3] 'The Social Function of Poetry', *The Adelphi*, July–September 1945.

always 'watching and waiting', and finally declaring themselves in the tongues of incandescent terror.[4] On the other side, neither in city nor in village is there a society 'keeping the rhythm in their dancing, as in their living' in an ordered 'concorde'. Instead, the individual is detached, a whirling bit of paper, or wandering in a bramble or a grimpen with no secure foothold, or lying awake trying to unweave, unwind, unravel, the tangle of its fate. And along with the busy travelling along material ways, the inorganic metalled roads, or the helpless unrelatedness of anxious insecurity, is the refusal to face any experience of the inner life—the torpor, the apathy, the 'silent funeral'; or what in prose Eliot has called 'the invincible sluggishness of imagination', which paralyses all movement, and repudiates all responsibility.

And over against these ways, all leading one way or another to death, the poet sets the creative pattern whose centre is life and peace; but whose way is never that of peace but always a sword. 'There is only the fight to recover what has been lost And found and lost again and again.' The parallel with the poet and his medium is exact: the achievement, the stillness, those moments when the sense of 'the complete consort dancing together' is felt as a reality; but the way, the actual moving, always the struggle:

With shabby equipment always deteriorating
In the general mess of imprecision of feeling,
Undisciplined squads of emotion.

The revelation of all this to the tribe, to make society and the individual share his own consciousness of it, is the poet's aim. And that again is another fight. Eliot has said[5] that it is inevitable that the man of letters should always be 'in a certain sense in opposition. He should be jealous to preserve the tradition of the culture of his people and of Europe: but in so doing he must constantly find himself opposed to current tendencies and popular values. All great literature is, in one aspect, a criticism . . . of the society in which the author lives. If he is not to criticize, he must remain silent.' Eliot's criticism probes very deep. . . .

While Eliot the prose writer asserts that heresy is diabolic and Catholic theology immutable, Eliot the poet provides us with just that refreshment and replenishment of symbolic approach which gives new meaning to old truths and reawakens the imagination to new growth. Its centre is Christianity, the traditional form of western culture, but a

---

[4] 'The old religions with their ridiculous—and horrible symbols, are not born out of the blue, but out of this very human soul that lives in us at this moment. . . . At any time they may break in upon us with destructive force, in the form of mass-suggestion, for example, against which the individual is defenceless. Our frightful Gods have only changed their names.' Jung, *Two Essays on Analytical Psychology*, p. 223.

[5] In an unpublished radio address given in October 1944 (Eliot House Collection, Harvard).

Christianity accepting its roots in cultures much older than itself, and recognizing itself not only in Dante and St John of the Cross, but in age-old 'pagan' symbols of the vitality of water, of fire, of earth, and age-old concepts of the communion and relatedness of the worlds of sense and of spirit; of the supersession of guilt by an understanding of the process of symbolic death and rebirth; and of the way of 'detachment' and contemplation as a path to the kingdom of God within. All this, and the truth that 'history is a pattern of timeless moments', and all the explorations into self-surrender and 'right action' which have led to that conclusion, provide 'revelation' indeed of profound realities, but realities whose acceptance does no violence to 'honesty and nature' and requires no supernatural sanctions. Eliot's prose sayings and his Anglo-Catholicism have perhaps blinded critics to the completely catholic, that is, universal character of his vision; to how 'at home' his conclusions are in *any* pattern of harmonious living; and how they strike home to the common roots of social and personal disorder at all times and among all peoples. . . .

When Eliot began to write, it was inevitable that his poetry should be 'undecipherable' to the reading public. The speech of the tribe had become impoverished, atrophied, inarticulate. Hence the return to some of the sources of its lost life, to the language of symbol, the logic of the imagination, made it appear a stranger, whose unfamiliarity must be repudiated. A generation of readers and critics and teachers, and of other poets writing in the same language, has done much to reawaken consciousness, and to widen the area over which the music can be heard. As to the fight for his values, all the poet can do in his art is to present them as poetry. 'The rest is not our business.'

From *T. S. Eliot: the Design of his Poetry*, Eyre and Spottiswoode, 1950, pp. 241–51.

D. S. SAVAGE

A Decline in Quality

. . . Mr Eliot's considerable reputation was earned first of all by his earlier work, and I may as well begin by saying that I see this writer's development as a poet to fall into two distinct parts. As I see it there is a qualitative difference between his earlier and his later work which, though few critics have thought it worth while to comment on, is surely, granting Eliot's importance, of some considerable significance.

Eliot's poetry and his prose writing have developed side by side. An early poetry of concentrated poetic value was accomplished by a fastidiously tasteful and sometimes slightly precious aesthetic criticism. But as he has grown older, the moralist in Eliot has developed somewhat at the expense of the aesthete. With his conversion to Anglo-Catholicism a pronouncedly religiose strain begins to be heard both in the prose and in the poems. From 'The Waste Land' (1922) and 'The Hollow Men' (1925) it is something of a jump to the contemplative tones of 'Ash Wednesday' (1930) and the succeeding poems. But while Eliot's later verse is interesting up to a point it lacks the integrity and the astringent personal quality of the earlier poems. To put it unequivocally, I see Eliot's poetic career from about 1925 as one of deterioration, if one can thus describe a process so sharply and clearly defined as the break between the one half of his work and the other.

Eliot's early poems, up to and including 'The Hollow Men', are unique in our literature. But besides being in itself a unique and valid achievement, which is of course its central and pivotal importance, his work of this period has meaning for literature as a whole, has meaning in relation to the continuity of the tradition of English poetry. Following the romantic movement of the early nineteenth century, and the enervated neo-romanticism of Tennyson, Browning and Swinburne, the pre-Raphaelites, and the poets of the *fin-de-siècle*, poetry as a whole, the idiom of verse which was shared by all the poets writing at that time, had ebbed to a low-water mark of flaccidity and nervelessness which it would be difficult to parallel from any period of English history. For the injection of a new and invigorating current, the renewal and tautening of this idiom, we are indebted in large measure to Mr Eliot's practice, following upon that of Ezra Pound; a practice which drew its strength from an acquaintance with contemporary French poetry, which had escaped the English dissolution in large measure, and from a by-passing of the English neo-romantic currents which made possible a fresh contact with English poetry of the most vigorous period. . . .

Eliot rejected both academicism and pomposity, and the quiet, sardonic, penetratingly realistic attitude he took and expressed, at first affronting the literate public, soon captured the imagination of his younger readers and, more than any other single influence, helped to bring poetry back to a serious confrontation of the actual world of daily experience.

This world of Eliot's is sharply and acridly *there*, intensely personal, intensely realized, particular and immediate. His descriptions are vividly unforgettable:

> Among the smoke and fog of a December afternoon
> You have the scene arrange itself—as it will seem to do—
> With 'I have saved this afternoon for you';
> And four wax candles in the darkened room,
> Four rings of light upon the ceiling overhead,
> An atmosphere of Juliet's tomb
> Prepared for all the things to be said, or left unsaid.
> We have been, let us say, to hear the latest Pole
> Transmit the Preludes, through his hair and fingertips.
> 'So intimate, this Chopin, that I think his soul
> Should be resurrected only among friends
> Some two or three, who will not touch the bloom
> That is rubbed and questioned in the concert room.'
> —And so the conversation slips
> Among velleities and carefully caught regrets
> Through attenuated tones of violins
> Mingled with remote cornets
> And begins . . .

So begins 'Portrait of a Lady'. And from this and other poems of that period one remembers the recurrent novel and startling phrases and evocations:

> Let us go then, you and I,
> When the evening is spread out against the sky
> Like a patient etherised upon a table; . . .

> Shall I say, I have gone at dusk through narrow streets
> And watched the smoke that rises from the pipes
> Of lonely men in shirt-sleeves, leaning out of windows? . . .

And if this is 'period-poetry', evoking the emotional quality of an unrecapturable past day, it is period-poetry of the most valuable kind, in which the emotional atmosphere is transformed into something permanent.

Superficially, we may say that the difference apparent between the early poems and the later is one of *environment*. Whereas Eliot first became recognized for his uniquely personal presentment of the squalor

B

and decay of the industrial metropolis and its soiled and banal humanity: whereas he was the acutely perceptive poet of 'The damp souls of housemaids/Sprouting despondently at area gates', of 'the hands/ That are raising dingy shades/ In a thousand furnished rooms' and the like, in the later poems this environment is passed over, like a disreputable associate of a misspent youth, for the rarer atmosphere of religious mediation and contemplation. But where the world of the early poems carries real and intense conviction, the atmosphere of the later verse, because of its intellectual rather than sensuous nature, fails to impose its reality sharply and definitely upon the reader's perceptions. The later verse, contemplative and refined, is lifted from the graphic presentment of actuality, and the poet's mind begins to work less concretely: in fact, less poetically. From the particular, Eliot passes to the generalized, observation and evocation, and the attempt to grapple this to the concrete actuality of experience, to endow it with authentic life, results in the strained impotence of the generalized image. Where Eliot tries determinedly to achieve concreteness in certain of his poems without this expedient, the attempt will lead him to the employment of archaic or biblical imagery, which is literary rather than actual: as in 'A Song for Simeon':

> Before the time of cords and scourges and lamentations
> Grant us thy peace.
> Before the stations of the mountain of desolation.
> Before the certain hour of maternal sorrow,
> Now at this birth season of decease,
> Let the Infant, the still unspeaking and unspoken Word,
> Grant Israel's consolation
> To one who has eighty years and no to-morrow. . . .

The loss of immediacy apparent in his later work, the substitution of the contemplative abstraction for the evocative imagery, is to be seen in such passages as this from 'Ash Wednesday':

> Because I know that time is always time
> And place is always and only place
> And what is actual is actual only for one time
> And only for one place
> I rejoice that things are as they are and
> I renounce the blessed face
> And renounce the voice
> Because I cannot hope to turn again
> Consequently I rejoice, having to construct something
> Upon which to rejoice. . . .

But perhaps one may best present Eliot's poetic declension by contrasting the earlier 'Preludes' with those short poems of his later period which follow upon the same structural pattern and appear in a certain

manner to be their counterpart. The force and economy of phrasing of
the brief 'Preludes' entitles them to comparison with verse of the order
of Shakespeare's songs. But compare this:

> The winter evening settles down
> With smell of steaks in passageways.
> Six o'clock.
> The burnt-out ends of smoky days.
> And now a gusty shower wraps
> The grimy scraps
> Of withered leaves about your feet
> And newspapers from vacant lots;
> The showers beat
> On broken blinds and chimney-pots,
> And at the corner of the street
> A lonely cab-horse steams and stamps.
> And then the lighting of the lamps.

with this:

> The wind sprang up at four o'clock
> The wind sprang up and broke the bells
> Swinging between life and death
> Here, in death's dream kingdom
> The waking echo of confusing strife
> Is it a dream or something else
> When the surface of the blackened river
> Is a face that sweats with tears?
> I saw across the blackened river
> The camp fire shake with alien spears.
> Here, across death's other river
> The Tartar horsemen shake their spears.

where the loss of concrete imagery and emotional immediacy is so
apparent as to require no comment.

Of the later poems, there remain the Choruses from *The Rock*, lines
with a didactic import originally printed in the context of a propagandist
pageant-play. Of these one can but say that they admirably serve their
purpose; some of them are solemnly impressive; they have not the
integral structure of *poems*. And lastly there is the sequence of long
poems which begins with 'Burnt Norton' and proceeds through 'East
Coker' and 'The Dry Salvages' to 'Little Gidding'.

It would be impossible to pretend that these poems are not, in their
way, impressive achievements. They bear the marks of deep sincerity,
of a mature intelligence and of experienced and conscientious craftsmanship. But despite all that has been claimed for them (and claimed, one
finds it impossible not to conjecture, mainly on the strength of Mr
Eliot's formidable reputation) they must be marked down as imperfectly

realized summaries of experience, as poetic failures. The dominant emotions conveyed by the early poems are those of weariness, boredom, frustration, self-doubt and dissatisfaction, but these qualities are brought within the crystallizing range of the poet's craftsmanship and are thereby mastered and transformed, made truly significant. The air of aridity, of weariness, which is exhaled by these later poems is marginal, is not part of the substance of the poetry itself, but is unintentional, arising from qualities which the poet has failed to bring in subjection to his inspiration. Morality in Eliot's mind having replaced art as the potential transforming agent of experience, a function which it is quite incapable of performing, the result is that Eliot's career oddly resembles, to make a theological comparison, a fall from the reign of Grace to the rule of Law. . . .

From *The Personal Principle*, Routledge and Kegan Paul, 1944, pp. 91–101.

The Early Poems

. . . It was Eliot in his essay on the metaphysical poets who first commented on the similarities between the English metaphysical and the French symbolist poets. And it is in *Prufrock and Other Observations* that the methods of these two schools are amalgamated, adapted and extended. The first simile in 'The Love Song of Alfred Prufrock'—

> Let us go then, you and I,
> When the evening is spread out against the sky
> Like a patient etherised upon a table;—

is a metaphysical conceit, an intellectual or 'wit' image, elaborated later in the poem:

> And the afternoon, the evening, sleeps so peacefully!
> Smoothed by long fingers,
> Asleep . . . tired . . . or it malingers,
> Stretched on the floor, here beside you and me.

These lines suggest that there is a kinship between Prufrock and the evening—peaceful, but artificially peaceful, and with an undertone of unhealthiness and unease—suggest even that the two are to be identified. This notion is intensified when the following lines from 'East Coker' are considered. They reveal much of the significance that the idea holds for Eliot:

> And you see behind every face the mental emptiness deepen
> Leaving only the growing terror of nothing to think about;
> Or when, under ether, the mind is conscious but conscious of
> nothing—

Prufrock and the evening are 'conscious but conscious of nothing', and Prufrock certainly, rapt in a monotonous routine, pondering his 'overwhelming question', which if it exists at all in any coherent shape will certainly, we feel, never be asked, must experience the 'terror of nothing to think about'. All this is involved in the first simile and in its relations to the rest of the poem. It is not altogether successful, for synthesis fails to result from the yoking together of the disparate ideas—we can see the relationship between the evening and Prufrock, who *is* the etherized patient, but are not convinced that this is sufficient to justify their being linked so violently together. There is a similar failure in this line from another poem—

> He laughed like an irresponsible foetus.
>   (*Collected Poems*, p. 31.)

Better is the comparison, in 'Prufrock', of the material 'streets', to the abstract 'arguments', for here the similarity is sufficient to suggest immediately the nature of the material. These images fall under both Johnson's definition of metaphysical wit—'a combination of dissimilar images, or discovery of occult resemblances in things apparently unlike'—and Edmund Wilson's analysis of symbolist technique—'The medley of images; the deliberately mixed metaphors; the combination of the grand and prosaic manners; the bold amalgamation of material with spiritual.'

More particularly may be mentioned the similarity in atmosphere between 'Prufrock' and these lines of Laforgue:

> Ah! que la vie est quotidienne.
> and   Tâchons de vivre monotone.

There is the same preoccupation with trivial routine,

> I have measured out my life with coffee spoons;[1]

the same desire to escape from any spiritual experience of a higher order than monotony—

> I should have been a pair of ragged claws
> Scuttling across the floors of silent seas.

the same delicately ironic expression. Prufrock, wandering by the sea and thinking of trivialities—'Do I dare to eat a peach?'—is aware that the mermaids will not sing to him, yet there is none of the desire implied in Donne's,

> Teach me to hear mermaids singing.

to which Eliot's lines seem to allude.

'Prufrock' begins with a highly selective piece of scene-setting, in which is established the character of the surroundings and incidentally of Prufrock. As there is an identity between Prufrock and the evening, so there is between him and 'the restless nights in one-night cheap hotels', the 'streets that follow like a tedious argument'. Each is unstable, shifting. We learn that Prufrock is undecided and vaguely troubled:

---

[1] A line such as this, with its swift transition from the grandiose 'I have measured out my life . . .' to the bathos of the finished statement, mingles 'the grand and prosaic manners', as Verlaine did in 'Le Faune', where the phrase,

> . . . cette heure dont la fuite
> Tournoie . . .

is completed by, 'au son des tambourins.'

And indeed there will be time
To wonder, 'Do I dare?' and 'Do I dare?'

. . . .

Do I dare
Disturb the universe?
In a minute there is time
For decisions and revisions which a minute will reverse.

The feeling of these lines is intensified if, as seems possible, we are
meant to recall Ford's,

Yet still a rumour of some novel fancy
Untasted or untried, puts off the minute
Of resolution, which should bid farewell
To a vain world of weariness and sorrows. . . .

If this is intended it is particularly interesting as showing Eliot's belief
in the necessity of suffering, a bidding farewell to the 'novel fancies', of
death even, as the essential precursor of spiritual rebirth. But this may
be no more than the tendency that afflicts all of us in reading this allusive
poetry, to see allusions that were not intended. In any case the aptness
of Ford's lines is indisputable, and that they are among those that have
impressed Eliot is shown by his quoting them in his essay on Ford
(*Selected Essays*. p. 195).

Eliot's conception of Prufrock's attitude to these 'novel fancies' is
perhaps best revealed by some consideration of the nature of Prufrock's
'overwhelming question'. It is justifiable to think of it as being the same
as the question asked in 'The Waste Land', (*Collected Poems*, p. 66).

What shall we ever do?

with its answer which answers nothing:

. . . The hot water at ten.
And if it rains, a closed car at four.

This answer pointedly avoids anything of true significance that is implied in the question: and so it is that Prufrock and the others accept
boredom—it is from fear that worse may ensue from an attempt to
probe too deeply.

This next re-expression of Prufrock's enervated indecision is again
allusive, to create a contrast, as with the oblique reference to Donne:

Would it have been worth while,
To have bitten off the matter with a smile,
To have squeezed the universe into a ball
To roll it toward some overwhelming question,

The allusion is to Marvell's

Let us roll all our strength and all
Our sweetness up into one ball,

And tear our pleasures with rough strife,
Thorough the iron gates of life.

('Coy Mistress.')

The contrasted philosophy, as well as the similarity of the formal
pattern, needs no emphasis. Prufrock never reaches a decision, never
penetrates beyond 'the cups, the marmalade, the tea', to a conclusion
either with the ladies in the poem or with his surroundings. The poem
ends with a reiteration of the desire to escape to 'the chambers of the
sea', beyond the complexities and troubles that may possibly be raised
by human associations. Prufrock does not see in the water symbol the
significance so often given it elsewhere in the poetry. For him it is only
a sufficiently remote place of escape.

Prufrock typifies all the characters in Eliot's first volume of poems.
He is essentially the same as Aunt Helen, who achieved significance
only with death, as the readers of *The Boston Evening Transcript*, as
Miss Nancy Ellicott with her futile modernity, as the 'damp souls of
housemaids'. Exception has been taken to this last phrase for no very
good reason. Although Eliot does not say so directly one is surely left
with the impression that Prufrock and the lady in 'Portrait of a Lady'
are equally afflicted with soul-dampness. Eliot is very far from attribut-
ing this exclusively to housemaids as a class: but they share in the
universal condemnation. Only Mr Apollinax, 'the resourceful man' as
we are told in the epigraph, is free from the taint. He is reminiscent of
'Priapus in the shrubbery', god of the fertility cults, and is associated
also with the life-giving water—

His laughter was submarine and profound
Like the old man of the sea's
Hidden under coral islands.

Here the significance given generally to the water symbol in Eliot's
poetry is elucidated by its being asosciated with fertility in the person
of Mr Apollinax.

The poem is concerned with the impact on the ultra-refined society
of Professor and Mrs Channing-Cheetah of someone possessing vitality,
whose talk still retains passion—a quality lacking in Eliot's other
characters. He is remembered as rich in significant associations, while
his hosts remain in the memory only as,

. . . a slice of lemon and a bitten macaroon.

Eliot tends to draw out of an image all the suggestion possible, and this
rapid association of ideas is well illustrated in 'Mr Apollinax':

I looked for the head of Mr Apollinax rolling under a chair
Or grinning over a screeen
With seaweed in its hair.

It is by the association of Apollinax with 'the worried bodies of drowned men', tugged by ocean currents, that this image is aroused. Its connection with the previous lines, though not overtly stated, is implicit, and this swift elaboration of the initial idea is equally a characteristic of metaphysical poetry.

Of the same nature as 'Prufrock' is 'Portrait of a Lady', which communicates the same 'slight sensation of being ill at ease'. It resembles, too, Ezra Pound's 'Portrait d'une Femme'. Pound's

> And bright ships left you this or that in fee.
> Ideas, old gossip, oddments of all things,
> Strange spars of knowledge and dimmed wares of price.
> Great minds have sought you—lacking someone else.
> You have been second always. Tragical?
> No. . . .

may be collated with the description of the 'bric-à-brac' in the lady's room in Eliot's poem, with her commonplace thoughts—

> Yet with these April sunsets, that somehow recall
> My buried life, and Paris in the Spring,

which impress as being no more than

> . . . things that other people have desired.
>   (*Collected Poems*, pp.18–19.)

And also with Prufrock's denial of tragedy—

> No! I am not Prince Hamlet, nor was meant to be;
> Am an attendant lord. . . .

All these are poems of a society concerned exclusively with trivial refinement, second-hand experience and complete spiritual inaction, although Pound does not reject the worth of his material.

In both 'Prufrock' and the 'Portrait' Eliot stresses the same social characteristics. In 'Prufrock'—

> There will be time, there will be time
> To prepare a face to meet the faces that you meet;—

and in the other—

> 'I shall sit here serving tea to friends,'
> And I must borrow every changing shape
> To find expression . . . dance, dance
> Like a dancing bear,
> Cry like a parrot, chatter like an ape.

In both it is the same trivial hypocrisy and dissimulation. Yet even in 'Portrait of a Lady' there is an advance, a glimpse of the way in which Eliot's moralizing will lead him. 'The Love Song' portrays a man indecisive, incapable of the vigorous decision of Marvell, or the conscious effort of Donne. As yet, however, there is no hint of the most serious implications of such spiritual indifference. These lines do give such a hint:

> Now that the lilacs are in bloom
> She has a bowl of lilacs in her room
> And twists one in her fingers while she talks.
> 'Ah, my friend, you do not know, you do not know,
> What life is, you who hold it in your hands';
> (Slowly twisting the lilac stalks)

Life, if it is lived as the lady and Prufrock live it, will be destroyed by them as surely as the lilac stalks which are also in their hands. In the slow deliberation of the last line is the first hint of the death-in-life theme that is to occupy so much of Eliot's later poetry.

That the people of these early poems are in essence the same as the inhabitants of 'The Waste Land' is shown by these lines from 'The Hollow Men':

> Let me be no nearer
> In death's dream kingdom
> Let me also wear
> Such deliberate disguises
> Rat's coat, crowskin, . . .

Again, the dissimulation, the suggestion by Eliot that the disguises adopted are animal-like. In this connexion we may recall a remark from Eliot's essay on Baudelaire: 'This means, I think, that Baudelaire has perceived that what distinguishes the relations of man and woman from the copulation of beasts is the knowledge of Good and Evil. . . .' In other words, without this perception, human beings are indistinguishable, spiritually, from animals,[2] and this is implied in the two poems already considered—particularly in 'Portrait of a Lady'. Primarily,

---

[2] The same idea is found in a later poem, 'Marina', in these lines:
> Those
> Who suffer the ecstasy of animals, meaning
> Death.

This poem, whose title directs our attention to the re-discovery theme in Shakespeare's *Pericles*, is concerned with spiritual rebirth. A contrast is implied between this play and Seneca's *Hercules*, from which the epigraph is taken, where the hero who has killed his children has suffered an irreparable loss, in that no re-discovery is possible. The influence of Baudelaire is discernable here too:

> . . . let me
> Resign by life for this life, my speech for that unspoken,
> The awakened, lips parted, the hope, the new ships.

The coupling of hope with the image of a ship recalls Baudelaire's making the ships in the harbour say, 'Quand partons-nous vers le bonheur?' As Eliot says in his essay on Baudelaire (*Selected Essays*, p. 390), this imagery has its origin in 'a dim recognition of the direction of beatitude'. The theme of Eliot's poem is greatly clarified by the knowledge that he is using the image of ships as Baudelaire did.

however, they are preliminary sketches of the society of 'The Waste Land', without the full moral implication of the later poem.

Phrase repetitions in 'Portrait of a Lady'—and in 'Prufrock'—lend to the conversational rhythm a sense of the repetitive quality, the boredom, of the lady's life:

> And how, how rare and strange it is, to find
> In a life composed so much, so much of odds and ends, . . .
> To find a friend who has these qualities,

The same is found in her speech on page eighteen of the *Collected Poems*, beginning, 'I am always sure that you understand', and its last line re-occurs as she says goodbye towards the end of the poem. As well as sustaining the atmosphere, this hesitant reiteration charges the conversational rhythm with a pattern that lifts it above exact reproduction of speech idiom. . . .

The swift changes of tempo in Eliot's poetry can be traced to the metrical precedents created by the French poets, as the frequently abrupt introductions to his poems are based on the example of some of Donne's opening lines: they are the same in kind as Donne's, but without the same vigour—as is of course suitable to Eliot's poetry.

Compare, for example, these opening lines: Donne's, 'For God's sake hold your tongue and let me love,' and Eliot's, 'Let us go then, you and I'. The relationship here is parallel to that between Eliot's tempo changes and those of Corbière. In 'Burbank with a Baedeker', these lines,

> The smoky candle end of time
>
> Declines. On the Rialto once.
> The rats are underneath the piles.
> The jew is underneath the lot.
> Money in furs. The boatman smiles,

recall the staccato effect of Corbière's,

> English spoken?—Espagnole? . . .
>   Batignolle? . . .
> Arbore le pavillon
> Qui couvre ta marchandise.
>   O marquise
> D'Amaégui! . . . Frétillon! . . .,
>
> ('Après la Plui.')

although Eliot's effects are not so extreme.[3]

[3] A closer parallel is that Eliot based his 'Mélange Adultère de Tout' on Corbière's 'Epitaphe pour Jean . . . Corbière, Philosophe' (subtitled, 'Epave Mort-Né'), taking the title from the first line of Corbière's poem. It is interesting that in the French original is a playing with the meanings of life and death:—

> Mort, mais pas guéri de la vie . . .
> Il mourut en s'attendant vivre
> Et vécut s'attendant mourir.

It must be mentioned that Eliot's formal patterns owe a great deal to the Jacobean dramatists, as well as to the symbolist poets; there is in fact a combination of the two practices. The Jacobeans loosened the texture of the blank verse that had preceded them, and some of Eliot's poems reveal a further experimenting with a basic blank verse pattern—of which there is a suggestion in 'Prufrock' and 'Portrait of a Lady'. It contrasts with such syncopated rhyming lines as,

> Oh, do not ask, 'What is it?'
> Let us go and make our visit.

The regular pattern breaks down completely with lines as short as,

> Do I dare,

and an interesting comment on Eliot's allusion to Marvell is that the last line of the four,

> To roll it towards some overwhelming question,

postpones the rhyme for the preceding line. All this enhances the effect of wandering indecision. A subtle use of the same deliberate disintegration occurs in 'Gerontion', where the regular structure dies away to the whining effect of:

> . . . Vacant shuttles
> Weave the wind. I have no ghosts,
> An old man in a draughty house
> Under a windy knob.

to be restored as, in a sudden access of energy, Gerontion tries to justify himself:

> After such knowledge, what forgiveness? Think now
> History has many cunning passages, contrived corridors
> And issues . . .

This alternation is sustained skilfully throughout the poem, and is an extension of the loosening apparent in the Jacobean blank verse. . . .

In the four 'Preludes', the Sweeney poems, and certain others among Eliot's early poems, can be discerned the background, the milieu, of 'The Waste Land'. It owes much to Baudelaire, to Verlaine, and to the Jacobean dramatists. Firstly, Baudelaire, who 'gave new possibilities to poetry in a new stock of imagery of contemporary life . . . the use of imagery of the sordid life of a great metropolis, . . . the elevation of such imagery to the first intensity—presenting it as it is, and yet making it represent much more than itself' ('Baudelaire': *Selected Essays*, pp. 387–8). This description from 'Rhapsody on a Windy Night'—

> Remark the cat which flattens itself in the gutter,
> Slips out its tongue
> And devours a morsel of rancid butter—

and

> The reminiscence comes
> Of sunless dry geraniums
> And dust in crevices. . . .

recall Verlaine's

> Toits qui dégouttent, murs suintants, pavé qui glisse,
> Bitume défoncé, ruisseaux comblant l'égout, . . .

and the first two lines of the same poem ('La Bonne Chanson', xvi) with their reference to 'Les platanes déchus' lining the pavement. It is noteworthy that Verlaine and Eliot, seeking something peculiarly suggestive of the squalor of the modern city, seize the one on trees, the other on flowers, both reduced from freshness to the condition of their surroundings. Similarly Eliot's description:

> Regard that woman
> Who hesitates towards you in the light of the door
> Which opens on her like a grin.
> You see the border of her dress
> Is torn and stained with sand,
> And you see the corner of her eye
> Twists like a crooked pin

is akin to Baudelaire's

> . . . Monstres brisés, bossus
> Ou tordus. . . .
> Sous des jupons troués, et sous de froids tissus.

This background of squalor is not, as MacNiece has suggested, a mere romantic décor. It is, as has been shown, intimately related to the people whom it surrounds. The fog, in 'Prufrock', in 'Portrait of a Lady', 'the brown waves of fog' in 'Morning at the Window'—predecessor of 'the brown fog of a winter dawn', 'the brown fog of a winter noon' in 'The Waste Land'—is so consistent a feature in Eliot's scene that one is justified in seeing in it something more than décor. This dusk, of dawn and of noon, of morning and of afternoon, is the dusk of Dante's limbo with which Eliot equates the modern city. The passage of 'The Waste Land' already examined suggests the way in which Eliot presents the setting as it is and yet makes it 'represent much more than itself'. The initial impulse comes from Baudelaire; its application is Eliot's alone. . . .

The background of the Sweeney poems is a 'cavernous waste shore', the sound of an epileptic's shriek, the plotting—in 'Sweeney Among the Nightingales'—of Rachael and 'the lady in the cape' against 'the man with heavy eyes'. The atmosphere of 'Sweeney Agonistes' is best suggested by these lines at the close of the play:

You dreamt you waked up at seven o'clock and it's foggy and it's
    damp and it's dawn and it's dark
And you wait for a knock and the turning of a lock for you know the
    hangman's waiting for you
And perhaps you're alive
And perhaps you're dead

It is partly the unthinking violence of modern life that this play
portrays—

Any man might do a girl in
Any man has to, needs to, wants to
Once in a lifetime, do a girl in.
                              (*Collected Poems*, p. 130.)

The importance of this aspect of the background of Eliot's poems has
perhaps been minimized. It has more than a suggestion of the violence
of the Jacobean drama. Eliot's own impressions of industrial civilization
combine with those of Baudelaire, Verlaine, Laforgue, while his background of indecision, incertitude and violence recalls that of 'the
broken fragments and systems' in Jacobean drama. Impressions of the
present are collated, compared and contrasted with a section of the past
to form a vital part of his poetry. Symbolist technique is adapted to
his purposes, and the work of individual symbolist poets helps to form his
conception of the essentials of modern life. In these is the source of his
atmosphere of boredom, futility and squalor, and his conception of the
modern malady—the inability to be either damned or saved: '... damnation itself is an immediate form of salvation—of salvation from the ennui
of modern life, because it at least gives some significance to living'
('Baudelaire', in Eliot's *Selected Essays*). With this is compared the
Jacobean drama, similar yet differing—equally violent but with significance implicit in its violence, being on the side of Good or of Evil and
so leading to a life of meaning, because of either damnation or
salvation. . . .

From *The Poetry of T. S. Eliot*, Routledge and Kegan Paul, 1952,
pp. 48–63.

Word Repetition in the Early Verse

One of the most noticeable features of Eliot's poetry is his repetition of words. In the period up to 'The Hollow Men', where a certain unity of tone and technique prevails, the effects of this are especially striking and can be usefully discussed in some detail. In addition to the rhetorical 'figures of repetition', the reader encounters various kinds of more general repetition, each with its particular function. The words may be concentrated in a single passage or scattered widely over the whole of the period, but in either case a kind of poetic diction is established. . . .

Eliot often repeats a word to give dramatic effect to its appearance in a new context. *Softly* in 'Sweet Thames, run softly till I end my song' ('The Waste Land', 183) has a lyrical and gentle sense, but a sinister and completely different association enters in 'A rat crept softly through the vegetation' (187); moreover, the idyllic note of the first quotation, once the linkage has been perceived, will be ironically qualified by memory of the *softly* later on. Another example can be found in the two uses of *lingered* in 'Prufrock', the one to describe the fog lying on the pools in drains, and the other to describe the speakers in the last lines of the poem, who 'have lingered in the chambers of the sea'. Other examples are the two uses of *pin* in 'Prufrock' and *whisper* in 'The Waste Land' (316, 389). Eliot uses the repetition to make an implicit ironic comment.

Another effect of repetition, opposite to the previous one, is the repetition of a few words in the same emotional contexts and hence with the same significance. The use of *empty* in 'The Waste Land' illustrates this; in all its appearances, the same sense of desolation sometimes mixed with triviality is present: 'The river bears no empty bottles, sandwich papers' (178); 'And voices singing out of empty cisterns and exhausted wells' (385); 'There is the empty chapel, only the wind's home' (389); 'In our empty rooms' (410). Similarly, *stirring* in the following example performs the same function: '. . . stirring/Dull roots with spring rain' (3–4); '. . . stirred by the air . . . stirring the pattern on the coffered ceiling' (89–93). The word in both contexts suggests a dull and useless motion; the roots are stirred a little by the spring; the synthetic odours are stirred by the freshened air which is outside; artificial patterns on the ceiling, as lifeless as the dull roots, are seemingly moved to no apparent end. *Stone* on its four occurrences in 'The Waste Land' (20, 24, 95, 324) has a connotation of aridity and desolation, and much the same is true of other repetitions in the poem, such as *little* (6–7; 329–330) and *clutch* (19–20; 174–175); they work unconsciously at first, and add even more to the unity of the poem when they are consciously recorded.

Often, however, the repetition of words with the same emotional force extends beyond the few recurrences previously considered, and it then establishes a predominant mood. Thus *twist* and its grammatical variations are repeated five times within the short space of 'Rhapsody on a Windy Night', and, together with the various contorted objects, create an atmosphere of horror. In general, words denoting either sadness or fracture tend to be repeated. *Broken* is used several times (22, 173, 303, 409, 417) in 'The Waste Land' where it combines with other repeated words in various forms such as *dry* (7, 24, 194, 225, 337, 342, 355, 391) and *dead* (title, 2, 23, 40, 55, 63, 68, 116, 160, 192, 246, title, 312, 328, 329, 339) to create an atmosphere of a shattered and arid world. Eliot, however, can vary the mood of his tone-colour, as in the eleven repetitions of *friend* and its various forms in 'Portrait of a Lady'; here the iteration establishes a mood of pathos, the obsession of the lady being established by her monotonous repetition of the word.

In the early verse as a whole, the repetitions of words are similar to those in single poems and generate the same effects. Statistics are unfortunately unavoidable, for in considering such a small section of poetry, less than fifty pages of relevant text, the exact amount of repetition is important. In this early period, then, *feet* is repeated 12 times; *dead*, 28 times; *dry*, 16 times; and *broken*, 16 times—besides similar though less frequently used words, such as *cracked* and *damp*. The repetition of these words in fairly uniform sequence builds up a general impression of a decaying and broken civilization, almost by the sheer amount. A select view of the world is thus established, for almost all the words bear the same adverse associations. Occasionally, of course, the sequence is broken: the pattern of the word *feet* is disrupted once, for example, in 'Mr Eliot's Sunday Morning Service': 'Still shine the unoffending feet' here is the opposite, say, of 'the yellow soles of feet' ('Preludes'); the former is Eliot's only reference to the past in a series of repetitions of the word. Again, *yellow*, a word used by Eliot only in the very early poems, has always a pejorative sense, except for the Whistler-like 'evening yellow and rose' in 'Portrait of a Lady'. But such a disruption of sequence is inconsiderable compared with the uniform associations of the others. *Brown*, another of Eliot's frequently used colour-words, is mentioned ten times and almost always to signify drabness, as with a brown fog, a desolate landscape, or a suggestion of physical distaste—the light brown hair of the woman Prufrock encounters and the man in mocha brown; the sequence is broken only once by the 'seaweed red and brown' in 'Prufrock', where no distaste is apparent. Besides, therefore, making the period as a whole more unified stylistically, Eliot by such repetitive patterns is giving an indirect comment on the world as he sees it.

Another important effect of repetition is structural. In a sense, all of Eliot's words which are used several times have this function; they provide a continuity throughout apparently different contexts. This is true both of single poems and of the period as a whole. Since, as I have already pointed out, words repeated in several poems are part of a repetition throughout the whole period, it follows that the poems are to that extent a unity; they are not isolated from each other but form sections of a whole. Some repetitions, however, seem especially effective in linking together different elements. Such a linkage is important in the poems considered separately. In her *T. S. Eliot: The Design of His Poetry* (New York, 1949) Elizabeth Drew has already called attention to the contrast between *antique* in one section of 'The Waste Land' and the same word in the following, very different section (p. 78); although the word appears in such different contexts (as with *softly*), it helps to link together the two apparently unconnected sections. The same linkage is perhaps even more evident when a word recurs with the same significance. The 'pub scene' in 'The Waste Land' is joined by the same 'literary' use of *sweet* to the opening of the 'Fire Sermon': 'Good night, ladies, good night, sweet ladies, good night, good night' (172), and 'Sweet Thames, run softly, till I end my song' (176). This structural effect derived from repetition is especially striking when the repeated word occurs in a climax; the force of the ending is then greatly increased. In 'Preludes', by using the *vacant lots* of Part I in the last line of the poem, Eliot hints that the 'ancient women' are as aimless as the withered leaves and newspapers; similarly, *twisted* in 'Rhapsody on a Windy Night' gains by the occurrence of *twist* in the final line. In a comparatively long poem such as 'The Waste Land', other structural features can be detected. Thus *mountains* occurs once in the opening lines of the poem (17), when the speaker is descending with a sense of freedom, and then not again until line 327, when the speaker is ascending in a long, painful journey, and the word is repeated eight times; a 'frame' is established by this means. Again, *only* is found in the first section (21, 24) and, except for one instance (195), is not found again until the last section, where it is repeated nearly a dozen times. Thus an anticipation of this last, very rhetorical section is given by the two uses of the word in the 'biblical' passage of section one. Another anticipation is given half-way through the poem by the *only* in section three, and in the seventy-eight lines in the last section the anticipations are realized by the many instances of *only*. This particular repetition, besides creating a formal and artificial mood by the sheer number of occurrences, suggests a certain limitation.

Finally, the effect of repeated synonyms may be considered. Thus a word such as *withered* in 'The Waste Land' falls within the synonym-group of *dry*. Often key-words are used several times as loose connectives which build up an image pattern. *Claws* in 'Prufrock' is closely followed by the synonym *fingers*; the latter thereby acquires a sinister note. The words may also be more varied and suggest something of Eliot's under-

c

current of meaning, as in 'Portrait of a Lady', where there is a synonym-group of burial and resurrection, consisting of such words as *tomb*, *soul*, *resurrection*, *bloom*, and *buried*.

Within the period as a whole, recurrent synonyms are to be found that describe the condition of the civilization of the time. A list of synonyms of vacuity, for example, may be compiled from poems as different as 'Preludes' and 'Conversation Galante':

> *vacant* lots (twice) ('Preludes'); *nothing* ('Rhapsody on a Windy Night'); *vacuity*, *inane* ('Conversation Galante'); *vacant shutters* ('Gerontion'); *nothing* ('The Waste Land', 40, 120, 122, 302, 304); *empty bottles* (177); *empty cisterns, exhausted wells* (385); *empty chapel* (389); *empty rooms* (410); *hollow men, hollow valley, empty men* ('The Hollow Men').

Eliot's Swiftian disgust with the human body is found in his many syno-nyms for *laugh* and *grin*, which seem to have obsessed him at this early stage. And words such as *smile*, *grin*, *chuckle* that might seem to make his verse quite jocular are transformed to the vulgar or sinister by the con-text; a grin is 'lipless', a chuckle is like that of a skeleton. These synonym-patterns seem to have had a symbolic value for Eliot. The different aspects of burning, for example, must have exerted a great fascination for him; time after time, the reader comes across smoke, lamplight, candles; over forty words and phrases may be found which belong to this category. Perhaps to Eliot, *burning* in various forms symbolized the transitory state of human life, a life that is lived among shadows, though it might be argued that such synonym-groups as *burning* represent a romantic, twilight view of reality.

It might be maintained that this insistent repetition is evidence of a restricted vocabulary, poverty of inspiration, even though a similar apparent poverty can be found in other great writers. But besides the particular effects already discussed, two general ones follow from the use of the same words many times. Firstly, by such repetition, a specific viewpoint in the flux of experience is presented; Eliot does not record without selection. His constant repetition of key words such as *broken*, *dead*, and *dry*, for example, creates a poetic diction of considerable intensity. Secondly, such a repetition gives a unity to his verse which at first sight it may seem to lack; similar words appear in different parts of it, so that the parts become intrinsically co-ordinated together and a complete body of work results. His work is not, as Yvor Winters once asserted, a mere fragmentary recording of disorder. In effect, the adjectives *formal* and *deliberate* are those which best describe this aspect of his verse. Eliot's verbal art lies beneath the apparent formlessness and in contrast to the disunified subject-matter. The insistent repetition of key words may even suggest that beneath the despair inherent in the sordid and chaotic material there is an aesthetic affirmation, denying in a sense the hopelessness of that with which the verse deals.

From *Essays in Criticism*, Vol. 16, No. 2, 1966, pp. 201–6.

JOHN B. VICKERY

Gerontion

T. S. Eliot's poem 'Gerontion' operates on four levels of subject and image—those of individual man, religion, nature, and history—which fuse into a single complex theme, that of a dying man who begins by denying his divinity as a man, but regains it, at least in some degree, when he loses 'terror in inquisition'. The personal or individual level of the poem serves as the focus for the other three levels: 'Here I am, an old man in a dry month,/ Being read to by a boy, waiting for rain.' As a result its significance is more transparent and is taken for granted more than the other levels. To all intents and purposes, an old man musing on his past and anticipating his future, which is death, constitutes an uncomplicated image and a straightforward topic. Yet Gerontion's stream-of-consciousness is not purely realistic nor merely a technical device calculated to extend the creative artist's insight into individual psychology. His mental processes, conscious and unconscious alike, create a world in which religious, natural, and historical events of different periods and times exist simultaneously; and the man becomes coterminous and synonymous with his world. Hence his death assumes wider and deeper implications. Death is inevitable not only for human beings but also for the animal, vegetable, and mineral worlds on which cultures and civilizations are founded. In the face of this fact Gerontion elaborates both his despair over his mortality and the true nature of that divinity who is both human and immortal. . . .

Gerontion . . . is more than simply a man whose mental paralysis is in itself a moral act, more than the willing victim of unbelief. He, like Virgil for Dante, acts as the Guide whose knowledge aids man in threading the 'cunning passages' and 'contrived corridors' of history, in exploring the religious mysteries, and in confronting the terrors of the natural world. He is the Old Wise Man possessed of both good and evil, light and dark aspects, whom Jung regards as the personification of the spiritual principle. . . .

Gerontion does have other than antagonistic associations with the hero. He is not the heroic protagonist, the saviour; but the maimed priest-king living in a personal waste land. As a consequence, all he can do is recount the legend of his old age.

Gerontion's regressive aspect has been linked with his inability to apprehend the Word swaddled with darkness, the darkness of his own mind. His light aspect appears in his witnessing the approach of Christ the tiger 'in the juvescence of the year'. He can regard with equanimity and even a certain amount of exultation the advent of Christ as the tiger, the avenging conqueror bringing the punishment anticipated by a guilt-ridden mind. In this his attitude underscores Christ's own: both recognize that there is no via media between Christ and Satan, salvation and damnation. The significance of the grammatical object in 'us he devours' cannot be overestimated, for it links Gerontion to Christ albeit only as a victim. To be consumed by Christ is an inverted communion, a communion of sacrifice to, rather than of, the deity. As a consequence, Gerontion is made aware of the fact that death can be a transitional state leading to rebirth. In its light he is to see that he has not been futilely engaged during his rehearsal of the individual's tragic vision of nature, history, and religion.

Against the inverted communion of Gerontion stands the perverted communion of Mr Silvero and the others:

In depraved May, dogwood and chestnut, flowering judas,
To be eaten, to be divided, to be drunk
Among whispers; by Mr Silvero
With caressing hands, at Limoges
Who walked all night in the next room;
By Hakagawa, bowing among the Titians;
By Madame de Tornquist, in the dark room
Shifting the candles; Fräulein von Kulp
Who turned in the hall, one hand on the door.

For them Christ the tiger is a subject for an aesthetic ritual which is a betrayal and corruption of the fundamental nature of the sacrifice that they celebrate. With the enactment of this communion, however, the fuller and more ironic implications of the tiger image begin to emerge. The tiger as seen by these people is Blake's beast of prey which is linked with the dragon and Cowering Cherub of the Bible. The fact that it is, according to Northrop Frye, 'representative of the bogies inspired by human inertia' underscores the point that it, Mr Silvero, and the rest are all products of mental apathy. With this the communion's original aim of establishing a bond between the deity and his worshippers and of replenishing the forces of life is totally perverted. Man is now bound to the god's sinister antagonist through communion with the evil of his own nature and, in consequence, is effecting a corruption of life and fertility. . . .

In contrast to this group, Gerontion, after being consumed by the tiger which is Christ, is able to see, if not act, outside his own ego. It is significant that the measure of insight achieved by Gerontion follows his contemplative analysis of history:

Think now
History has many cunning passages, contrived corridors
And issues, deceives with whispering ambitions,
Guides us by vanities. Think now

She gives when our attention is distracted
And what she gives, gives with such supple confusions
That the giving famishes the craving.

History is found to be the senses and body of humanity. Its 'cunning passages, contrived corridors' are the general and macrocosmic form of the individual's senses which engage in a 'thousand small deliberations'. The 'pungent sauces' with which the physical man is tantalized are balanced on the mental level by 'vanities' and 'whispering ambitions'. In both cases, the result aimed at is a compounding of confusion and a paralysis of decision. On the level of history, the temptation motif, inaugurated by the epigraph, is recapitulated in concepts such as ambition and vanity, just as it is presented through images on the natural level. The two levels meet through being focused on religion and the figure of the man-god capable of rebirth after death. In the natural images—the goat, the tiger, the field, the house—there is an attempt to intimidate, to overawe, and to frighten Gerontian through the exhibition of the naked power of mortality. In history and its concepts, however, the destruction of Gerontion is sought through temptation and confusions of the issue. Naturally enough, then, history is presented as feminine, as the temptress seeking to lure men to their destruction. But until his conquest by the divine man, Gerontion saw Clio only as an old woman living in the rear of his house and 'poking the peevish gutter' of the past. She, like the natural world, depends for her vitality and regeneration on the religious imagination which sees existence in terms of incarnation and communion.

Yet at the same time history is the source of man's salvation in so far as it contains and records the recurring presence of the mystery of death and life which is concretely embodied in the figure of the dying and reviving god. It is this, then, that history gives to mankind. That there is a god, an incarnate deity, is accepted by man, a point dramatically rendered by Gerontion's reliving of the Nativity. The problem is that of determining the nature and authenticity of the various forms or manifestations of the divinity. So viewed, the ambitions and vanities history presents may be the temptation to exalt oneself as the god whom men are to worship. It is the risk that Christ took, and it is appropriate therefore that it should be the first facet of the problem to be confronted by Gerontion. Related aspects, however, are presented following each recurrent 'think'. Thus, history is next seen by Gerontion not only to give a deity to men when their minds are diverted to mundane issues, but also to give a plethora of deities so that the craving for the one God goes unsatisfied and ultimately dies.

Yet not only is too much given, also the deity has in the course of history appeared both too soon and too late:

Gives too late
What's not believed in, or if still believed,
In memory only, reconsidered passion. Gives too soon

Into weak hands, what's thought can be dispensed with
Till the refusal propagates a fear.

Since the attitude of 'reconsidered passion' reflects that of Gerontion in
the early part of the poem, it is clear that it is meant to characterize the
manner of ageing persons and cultures, of which the contemporary
world is an instance. By implication, Christ is the object of worship who
was given too late, the last of a long line of dying gods; hence, people,
wearied from attempting to determine the true god among the Adonises,
Osirises, and Attises of the world, are no longer capable of a literal,
fervent, and immediate acceptance. They, like Gerontion, have lost the
ecstasy of assent. On the other hand, what was given too soon were the
pagan deities, such as those just mentioned, whose priests and
worshippers were unprepared to follow out the implications of the god's
appearance in history. Thus, Gerontion, like the pagans, finds the
refusal of the age to contemplate the miracle of Incarnation giving birth
to a fear that there is no true god. In this state of mind, the idea of
rebirth and regeneration does not exist; death becomes the mad,
whirling, fractured atoms of annihilation encountered by De Bailhache,
Fresca and Mrs Cammel.

The ultimate facet of Gerontion's dilemma is embodied in his
recognition of the inescapable nature of age and mortality:

Think
Neither fear nor courage saves us. Unnatural vices
Are fathered by our heroism. Virtues
Are forced upon us by our impudent crimes.
These tears are shaken from the wrath-bearing tree.

Neither fear nor courage can restore the hope for immortality nor the
faith of resurrection. Heroism leads to the Satanic vice—pride in stoic
resistance; the criminal refusal of belief conversely forces man into the
virtue of enduring what he has occasioned. The tears shaken from the
wrath-bearing tree are the knowledge of this essential human dilemma,
of man's loss of divinity and immortality and of his having to endure
death if he would regain them. In bearing wrath, the tree not only
suffers for the knowledge of mortality man has gained from it, but also
produces wrath as its fruit, thereby revealing itself as the vegetable
analogue of the conquering Christ. It is the form beneath which timid
and straitened imaginations have hidden the dying and reviving god
whom men must share in communion if they would live eternally.
History sees man and religion as natural: the revolutionary implications
of the Word are disguised as a dangerous animal and a poisonous tree.

With the recognition of this, Gerontion accepts the necessity of
destroying and surrendering his old life as a prelude to a new existence
which is, in effect, a new time: 'The tiger springs in the new year. Us
he devours.' The suggestion that he is merely waiting for the end is
replaced by the realization that death is not the end for men: 'Think at

last/ We have not reached conclusion, when I/ Stiffen in a rented house.'
Neither life nor the contemplation of it is without purpose; existence
is teleological and replete with its own power: 'Think at last/ I have not
made this show purposelessly/ And it is not by any concitation/ Of the
backward devils.' In disclaiming the assistance of 'the backward devils',
Gerontion is assuming full responsibility for his life. With true Augus-
tinian asceticism he recognizes that the body and its senses are useless
hindrances to the union of man with God, and in this recognition lies
his acceptance of his old age and mortality:

> I have lost my sight, smell, hearing, taste and touch:
> How should I use them for your closer contact?
>
> These with a thousand small deliberations
> Protract the profit of their chilled delirium,
> Excite the membrane, when the sense has cooled,
> With pungent sauces, multiply variety
> In a wilderness of mirrors.

By striving to 'protract the profit' of their existence, the senses merely
endeavour to postpone the inevitable loss which is a necessary stage in
the cycle of rebirth. Each sense is an illusion and each reflects from the
one to the other thereby multiplying their own variety and hiding
the single fact of death, which is really a crisis symbol suggesting the
necessity of freeing oneself from desire.

Gerontion ironically shatters this sensuous illusion by the question
'What will the spider do,/ Suspend its operations, will the weevil/
Delay?' For man, time is the impersonal equivalent to his personal
mortality; as such, its effects are those of physical dissolution and a
falling from the memory of mankind. From this confrontation of
mortality on a conceptual level, Gerontion then passes to envisaging
frankly and without evasion two concrete images of the way in which
man can conclude his life:

> De Bailhache, Fresca, Mrs Cammel, whirled
> Beyond the circuit of the shuddering Bear
> In fractured atoms. Gull against the wind, in the windy straits
> Of Belle Isle, or running on the Horn,
> White feathers in the snow, the Gulf claims,
> And an old man driven by the Trades
> To a sleepy corner.

The first of these is that of total and irrevocable destruction, a bursting
into fragments, which overtakes all those who see death as a *terminus
ad quem* rather than as a transitional state protected by sacred rites. It is
perhaps no accident that this fate befalls man in the vicinity of that
planet which was associated with Typhon, the fratricidal slayer of
Osiris, the dying and reviving god. In contrast to the first, the second

image, that of the natural and human worlds submitting to the Gulf, conveys the sense of some underlying continuity which provides a perennial renewal of life through death. In seeing himself and everything of which he is a part returned to water, Gerontion recognizes that the apparent threatened return of chaos is in reality a prelude to Genesis and the divine creation upon which every man's existence is contingent. By the same token he does not flinch when the Gulf by its abyss-like nature calls up the notion of sin and man's capacity for depravity, nor when as a whirlpool it mocks him by aping the tortuous, circular manner of his own mental processes.

These threats and dangers no longer paralyse him with apprehension, for he sees now that they are the products of a sterile mind which itself is the inevitable consequence of age and mortality. And though both brain and season are dry, yet this too is but one of a series of states and not an eternal condition for human existence. With the articulation of this view, Gerontion has carried his musings on mortality and immortality to their logical conclusion. At the beginning of his reverie, he saw age as itself a kind of death, but toward the end of the poem the inevitability of death is balanced by the possibility of rebirth. In effect, the entire poem charts Gerontion's gradual awareness of his own nature and state of mind. From 'Here I am, an old man in a dry month' to 'Tenants of the house,/ Thoughts of a dry brain in a dry season' encompasses the development: from personal self-dramatization to impersonal recognition and assessment. Like the mourners in 'The Waste Land', he has learned to die 'with a little patience'. And in the last analysis, what gives him that patience is the knowledge of his incapacity for any other action than that of knowledge.

From *Arizona Quarterly*, Vol. 14, No. 2, 1958, pp. 107–15.

GEORGE WILLIAMSON

The Structure of *The Waste Land*

I

The paradox of the seasons, with which the poem begins, inverts the normal attitude towards the life-cycle, thus reversing the significance of the vegetation myth and giving an ironic turn to the office of 'The burial of the dead'. Spring disturbs the dead land, stirring memory and desire; winter lets it forget. Then the verse modulates into narrative, the stirred memory that illustrates and supports this attitude. Summer caught them unaware (surprised them), coming with rain. If it were not for the opening lines, this would seem little more than an international episode—a memory of another spring. In this garden scene Marie is introduced by the German, 'I am not Russian, I come from Lithuania, pure German'. Her desire for the mountains is mixed with a memory of fear, and her life is a retreat.

But what are the dull roots to be stirred by rain? The son of man cannot answer because he knows only the Waste Land, which here suggests both the death imagery from Ecclesiastes and the fear 'of that which is high', illustrated in Marie. Here Ecclesiastes, chapter 12, blends images of Isaiah, chapter 32, and Luke, chapter 23: latent in the 'dead tree' and the 'red rock'—the colour of 'The fire sermon'—is the burial of Christ, which involves the preserver of the Grail and brings the journey to Emmaus in Part V. The speaker, who often echoes the prophetic note, will show man something different from the shadow of time in this land; he will show him 'fear in a handful of dust'. If this image begins with the biblical association, it ends in the vegetation myths. And again we get a garden scene, framed by the sailor's melancholy song in *Tristan*,[1] a story of tragic passion. The question 'where lingerest thou?' is finally answered by 'desolate and empty the sea'. But the garden scene accounts for the answer. The capitalized Hyacinth suggests the vegetation god and a victim of love. The protagonist's response is striking: a failure of speech and sight, a state neither living nor dead describing the effect of the vision of the Grail upon the impure. A love-death would be appropriately framed by snatches of song from Wagner's *Tristan und Isolde*, but the sea in itself expresses a sufficient

---

[1] The opening German has been translated thus:

Fresh blows the wind from off the bow,
My Irish maid, where lingerest thou?

change. The German carries us back to the scene with Marie and amplifies its associations.

Eliot's references to the present scene in Part II make it very important. Its final meaning, what is to be discovered in 'the heart of light, the silence', remains to be seen. Let us remember that we were to be shown fear; the associations of this experience acquire a new setting in the fortune. For the moment we may venture this statement: the initial state of mind is defined by the experience of spring followed by the experience of the Waste Land; 'the roots that clutch' in both are those of fear, and their origin is found in the 'Hyacinth garden'.

The speaker's need of clairvoyance introduces Madame Sosostris; perhaps she can look into the silence and interpret. She is a psychic fortune-teller, but she has a bad cold, which may hamper her powers; nevertheless, her wisdom is the best there is, involving a malicious pack of cards. The fortune itself has already entered our discussion, and accounts for the rest of the poem; but some details may be observed. In general her limitations, and the irony of the poem, appear in what she does not see. Her clairvoyance does not extend to an identification of the protagonist with Ferdinand, but only with the drowned Phoenician Sailor; yet the line from *The Tempest* which suggests this identification also connects the 'pearls that were his eyes' with the preceding experience, 'my eyes failed'. Of course this is a transformation image, which in the present context is committed to death. The irony of her shortcomings is more apparent in the failures to see which she mentions. In fact, the voice of irony begins to be heard in this section. In terms of these cards (but not of the initial attitude) there is none greater than to 'fear death by water'. If 'dear Mrs Equitone' is the lady of nerves in Part II, we may add to the irony. Certainly we must not forget it in the line, 'One must be so careful these days'—lest this wisdom fall into the wrong hands. But the fundamental irony is the restoration of a greater meaning to life by means of this 'wicked pack of cards'.

Henceforth this fortune and the experience which it interprets colour the vision of the protagonist. Although he has become one of the dead— 'I had not thought death had undone so many'—the city appears 'unreal' to him as it does not to them. They do not share his misgivings about the Waste Land; they are not conscious of the cruelty of April, or of 'a dead sound on the final stroke of nine' (Luke 23:44). He not only confuses but mingles his fortune with their reality. This explains the illusionary aspect of the poem, which assumes the Hamlet mask of irony or madness when the apparent contrast seems too great. Death echoes through this section until it culminates in 'That corpse you planted last year in your garden'. You do not plant corpses, except in vegetation ceremonies; and we are reminded of the 'Hyacinth garden', of the slain Hyacinth and the garden experience. The taunting questions about the expectation of growth intimate that this was not so much a planting as 'the burial of the dead'. And the 'hypocritical reader', as well as Stetson and the speaker, engaged in this planting of the corpse which evokes the corn-god Osiris, the scattered god of resurrection, and suggests the Hanged Man, whom the Madame did not find. The sardonic tone of the speaker has behind it not only this awareness but the weight of his own experience in the garden, of his attitude towards the seasons, and of his fortune. The corpse of the garden appears again in Part V, where this theme is openly resumed.

But one or two details in this section cannot be ignored. When the protagonist mentions 'the ships at Mylae', he is associating himself, appropriately enough, with the Phoenician Sailor in a famous engagement of the Punic Wars. We should note the associations with the sea and things Phoenician in the poem; they are part of the protagonist's inheritance. The 'Dog' is more important than Eliot's transformation of Webster; rather, it is the transformation, for it develops the ambiguity of the planted corpse. If Dog involves Sirius—as in 'Sweeney among the nightingales'—he becomes a sign of the rising of the waters and is friendly to growth. But Dog may also involve Anubis, a watcher of the dead who helped to embalm the broken Osiris. By his ambiguity the Dog presents an ironical aspect, and this irony centres in the intent of the planting, which explains the 'hypocrite lecteur' and his ambiguity as both subject and object. We must not ignore Eliot's use of capitals. As a source the dirge in *The White Devil* (V, iv) is significant because it provides a suggestive parallel and contrast with the dirge from *The Tempest*, which describes the drowned Phoenician Sailor; and because it belongs to a scene which recalls the mad Ophelia and includes a ghost with a flower-pot containing 'A dead man's skull beneath the roots of flowers'. This is Eliot's most Websterian poem, especially in the imagery. And let us observe that the ironic close which is found in Part I is repeated in other parts. If the Dog and the Hyacinth garden generalize the memory of 'Dans le restaurant', they illustrate the extension of that poem.

II

Of the rich allusiveness of the opening section of Part II, much is indicated in the notes, and much has been said. In its opulent detail 'the lady of situations' issues from a long past into a luxurious present. Cleopatra and Dido suggest her varied fortunes, and their splendour surrounds her, touched now and then by a sly detail like the parenthesis. Most insinuating, however, are 'her strange synthetic perfumes', which 'troubled, confused and drowned the sense'; for here we are in the presence of Belladonna, no less narcotic than cosmetic, herself presently in need of an anodyne. But as a Siren she is more than a parody of Pater's Mona Lisa. The pictured 'change of Philomel', whose place in Part III is indicated by a note, introduces another significance in the suggestion of violation survived by the 'inviolable voice,'

And still she cried, and still the world pursues,
'Jug, Jug' to dirty ears.

The chase has not ceased, and the nightingale's sounds are both representative Elizabethan and associative modern. If the other pictures are 'withered stumps', like Philomel's tongue, they come into the class of 'broken images'; but at least provide an inclination, 'leaning, hushing the room enclosed'. As someone approaches, the lady's hair becomes a sensuous and irritable image of her mood.

As she speaks we are reminded of the garden experience, for her questions counterpoint 'I could not speak'. The protagonist is thinking about 'rats' alley', the waste alley of death; and a note connects it with Part III. If the borrowing from Webster's *Devil's Law-Case* (III, ii) is looked up, it will only reinforce the Websterian character of this scene. But the wind's part in this poem bears inspection. The questions about knowing, seeing, and remembering nothing play over past details as the memory comes. We remember 'my eyes failed . . . and I knew nothing' as he recalls his 'death'; and a note connects it with the garden and fortune. Of course his replies puzzle the lady until she asks if there is nothing in his head. And he answers, nothing 'But O O O O that Shakespeherian Rag'—only the tune of Ariel's dirge. While he mocks, she becomes the image of distraction; and her ultimate question is answered by his derisive but grim summary of the daily boredom waiting for the final knock. Eliot's reference to Middleton's play merely emphasizes the game of chess as a cover for seduction, especially for 'the lady of situations' in the upper class.

The change of speech in the next section immediately places the scene on a lower level of society. But to place it in a 'pub' or tavern, we need to recognize 'Hurry up please it's time' as the words which announce it's closing time. This scene makes explicit, without the reticence of the other's game, what is meant by 'a good time'. And it does this in verse that not only catches the inflections of the lower class, but shows time hurrying it along instead of hanging upon its hands. The problem which appears in Lou's or May's gossip comes to a climax in the question, 'What you get married for if you don't want children?' It puts 'a good time' against a background of the frustration of life, and modulates the death theme to this level. The final 'good night'—ironic in its elegant, ceremonious contrast—is in the language of the first scene, and derives from Ophelia's mad farewell (Hamlet, IV, v); hence the protagonist did not stay with the lady of nerves, but is still mocking the lady of situations with bits of 'Shakespeherian Rag', as he recalls another death by water. If this is a very economical rounding-off of both scenes, it is not a departure from Eliot's manner of making his speaker identify himself, and certainly not from the particular means of discrimination employed in this part.

III

'The Fire Sermon' not only extends 'A Game of Chess' but exposes its moral significance. It is developed likewise in terms of the obsessions which derive from the protagonist's fortune. What haunted his mind in the previous part now centres his vision 'death by water', which is associated with the characters that develop its ominous implications. Here we find the Merchant who melts into the Sailor and 'the Lady of the Rocks', but in the midst of all the river. The dead season has come to the river; its canopy of leaves is broken:

> the last fingers of leaf
> Clutch and sink into the wet bank.

And so do all who live by this river, which ultimately flows into the sea that drowns the Phoenician Sailor. The 'Sweet Thames' refrain, which derives from Spenser's 'Prothalamium', reminds us of 'A spousall verse' and announces another song. The title has warned us that there is a sermon in the song, and both indicate that this part will be more evocatory than dramatic.

After the reminder of Spenser, the description of the river suggests that his song is being rewritten in a modern key; and this suggestion is reinforced by the transition from the 'nymphs' to their 'friends', who have been casual indeed, 'left no addresses'. Then comes the sudden revelation, both of the waters and the mood:

> By the waters of Leman I sat down and wept. . . .

This line is reinforced by remembering Psalm 137: 'By the rivers of Babylon, there we sat down, yea, we wept, when we remembered Zion.' But why the change to 'Leman'? Not because it is the old name for Lake Geneva, but because it is an old name for 'lover'. Water in the modern Waste Land is a negative element, a river of lust. After this apparent but not real *non sequitur*, he reinvokes the Thames. The request to 'run softly till I end my song' may acquire further meaning.

The next lines, after the method of this poem, identify the speaker by his thought. The sounds of death haunt the protagonist with whom we have been concerned. He is not the poet, unless we choose to ignore all of his efforts to project a character by means of a series of illusory characters. Now he hears Marvell's figure of time as a figure of death, and is once more in 'rats' alley' as the one who wept at Ariel's dirge. But Ferdinand is modernized; he is not merely

> Sitting on a bank
> Weeping again the King my father's wrack.

And he is also more ancient than Ferdinand; he belongs to the line of Fisher Kings. It was while sitting on this bank that Ferdinand heard Ariel's dirge—now fixed in the protagonist's mind by its association with the Phoenician Sailor. Before long he echoes the line which completes this quotation, but meanwhile much has intervened to reinterpret 'this music'.

But at his back he hears other sounds—or are they different? They are the sounds of the city, but in a familiar pursuit. They are the modern sounds of hunting, of lust; whether it is 'Actaeon to Diana', or 'Sweeney to Mrs Porter', it is the old game of Tereus and Philomel. To the protagonist, whether he would be a Parsifal or is to be a Fisher King, washing the feet is a spring rite in another sense; for it preceded the restoration of the Fisher King and was accompanied by the singing of children in the choir loft ('And O! the voices of children singing in the choir'). The irony belongs to his vision: water has lost its proper efficacy, has become malignant. But he hears other sounds not less disparate— the song of rape belonging to the nightingale, already introduced.[2] 'Unreal City' indeed to such a vision, to a mind concerned with the Fisher King! Of course the implication is that it lacks true reality.

Whether the name of the Merchant plays on the meaning of 'well-born' or not, he is now unkempt; and reminds us, particularly by his vulgar French, of the old waiter in 'Dans le restaurant'. Perhaps that poem has given us both the Merchant and the Sailor, who coalesce. If he has made improper advances to the protagonist, which would support the general lust theme, he is still the trader; and business is probably the rival mystery which the Madame is forbidden to see, despite her discreet 'Thank you'. This would explain the use of cryptic business terms. Of course they may be subordinate to the 'currants' as dried vestiges of the Bacchic cults, and thus part of an initiation into similar orgies, or merely of an initiation into the modern ritual. . . . But 'profit and loss' is an important sign in the mergence of Merchant and Sailor, and must not be discounted even as a Phoenician lust. And the loss of vision passes from the garden to the fortune to this embodiment.

If the sequence carries us from the 'one-eyed' to the blind, it does not leave the hunt of lust in the city; and if the protagonist has now been qualified in the knowledge of both sexes, he is ready to assume the role of Tiresias. He has already sounded the prophetic note 'by the waters of Leman' and the 'motors' now pass into the 'human engine', which expresses itself mechanically. 'I Tiresias' is the only explicit identification of the speaker in the poem, and there is a reason for it. He is not a character in the fortune; but he is the supreme metamorphosis that brings together all the metaphoric transformations and thus is qualified to summarize their experience. 'What Tiresias *sees*, in fact, is the substance of the poem', but not the whole poem.[3] This departure from fortune is therefore identified. And for the protagonist the sexual quali-

[2] See Trico's Song in Lyly's *Campaspe*:

What bird so sings, yet so does wail?
O! 'tis the ravished nightingale.
Jug, Jug, Jug, Jug, Tereu, she cries,
And still her woes at midnight rise.

[3] A later statement of what he sees is found in the essay on Baudelaire, *Selected Essays*, p. 344.

fications of Tiresias have a deeper meaning than prophetic power: he, 'though blind', is 'throbbing between two lives', one dead, the other powerless to be born. But, like Tiresias, he can see the nature of the 'dead'; his vision springs from similar experience.

The introduction of 'the typist' illustrates Eliot's device of syntactic condensation; functioning as both object and subject, she exemplifies the metamorphic flow of things in this poem. The typist scene repeats on still another level, and still more openly, the 'game of chess' episode; but, more significantly, it interprets overtly this experience for the participants. They are apathetic, both morally and emotionally—human machines. The role of Tiresias is also appropriate to the protagonist because he is now walking 'among the lowest of the dead'. Finally the modern significance of this act is registered in the reaction of the typist; the 'gramophone' makes it also mechanical. The 'automatic hand' has already appeared, with a similar implication, in 'Rhapsody on a Windy Night.' Of course the shift in values is projected by the parody of Goldsmith's song; in that poem, 'When lovely woman stoops to folly', her only art is—to die. Both likeness and difference are responsible for the irony.

'This music crept by me upon the waters'—it is a synoptic music, amplifying Ariel's dirge; and the speaker is once more Ferdinand. This music transports him to another music in the haunts of fishermen—he is one too—near the church of Magnus Martyr; the collocation becomes more than geographical, whether in a biblical or a Fisher King context. What the church holds is 'inexplicable', but not unhinted; its colours bear watching in the next section. Here 'in Lower Thames Street' he hears the Thames song; now it runs less softly.

The change of verse form provides the transition, but it is not unexpected because of the early distinction between his song and that of the Thames. Of course, the notes state this transition to the Song of the Thames-daughters (the departed 'nymphs') and further indicate that the three speak in turn lines 292 to 306 inclusive. But without this knowledge little would be missed, since their story is the same story. The two opening stanzas, or the song as distinct from its story, contrast present and past scenes of the river, which are centered in 'barge' and 'shell'. Both craft are marked by 'red', but white and gold are absent in the first scene and distributed in the second. In the modern scene Ionic 'white and gold' hold an inexplicable splendour in the church, perhaps suggestive of the Grail. And since these are the waters of Babylon, Zion may be suggested by Magnus Martyr. The chorus might be recognized by an opera-goer, but we also have the note. This refrain of the Rhine-daughters in *Götterdämmerung* ('the judgment of the gods') laments the loss of the Rhinegold or beauty of the river; it performs a similar function here, for other guardians of the gold; and again the poem returns to Wagner to express a theme of desolation. Elizabeth and Leicester both figure in Spenser's *Prothalamium* and give continuity to the 'affairs' of the river, not to its drift and pollution.

As the Thames-daughters recount their story, we learn that they, like the Rhine-daughters, have been violated. The scene carries them down the river to the sea, and the moral journey is similar, ending in a state that 'can connect Nothing with nothing', that calls its violation merely the 'broken fingernails' of people who expect nothing. The syncopation of the chorus to that flippant, modern 'la la' repeats the last ironic echo of the gramophone.

But 'the waters of Leman' flow on; 'red sails' still carry the Leman, like St Augustine, to Carthage. The protagonist finishes the song which he has heard, connecting it with meaning, in which it has failed; for Carthage, like Mylae, was familiar to the Phoenician Sailor, his card. Now the sermon enters the song of the Thames. We can read the 'burning' line without becoming aware of Buddha's Fire Sermon, but not without being aware of its theme of passion or lust. And we do not need to know St Augustine in order to know out of what the Lord plucks—out of this burning or these waters. It may help to know that St Augustine said: 'I entangle my steps with these outward beauties, but Thou pluckest me out, O Lord, Thou pluckest me out'; or that Buddha preached that moral regeneration begins by 'conceiving an aversion' for the lusts of the flesh; but these details merely amplify the significance of 'burning' that is already in the poem.

Eliot's notes are interesting for his evaluation of his sources, but they are important chiefly for their emphasis on the collocation of Buddha and St Augustine. In terms of the poem, theirs is a better wisdom than that of Madame Sosostris, and it is the same for both. The impact which their wisdom loses by reason of poetic economy, it recovers by virtue of its culminating position, which has the whole weight of the lust theme behind it. The syntactic ambiguity of the final 'burning' suggests, of course, that burning may define the means by which one is plucked as well as the state from which one is plucked. As the river's song ends on the theme of being plucked out, we may recall the introduction:

> the last fingers of leaf
> Clutch and sink into the wet bank.

And so they clutch and sink into the waters of Leman unless they are plucked out.

IV

When 'Death by Water' is executed in Part IV, it marks the end of the journey on 'the waters of Leman', the ultimate fear represented by the 'drowned Phoenician Sailor'. It rewrites the dirge which associated Ferdinand with the Sailor, and does so with the conclusion that finished a similar sequence of experience for the old Phoenician waiter in 'Dans le restaurant'. This is the negative issue for such experience. It is

D

significant that this is the only part without notes—the earlier note
belongs to the second St Augustine allusion at the end of Part III;
here the poet is his own source, his own explanation.

This part describes the usual way of becoming free from the fire of
passion, not the way of self-discipline. Here the Sailor is deprived of his
lust for the 'outward beauties' and the 'profit and loss'. Sea currents pick
the lust from his bones, and he reverses the course of his life as he enters
the vortex. There may be a reminiscence here of the sea-dogs of Scylla
and the whirlpool of Charybdis; or of Virgil's allusion (*Eclogue VI*) to
Scylla's whirlpool and her sea-hounds that destroyed sailors. This
conclusion now finds it unnecessary to say, 'it was a painful fate', but
necessary to add to the injunction,

> Gentile or Jew
> O you who turn the wheel and look to windward.

And with this addition comes the 'Wheel'—of fortune or fate as well as
of ships—which appeared in the fortune. If the epitaph says, with
Edmund in *King Lear*,

> The wheel is come full circle; I am here,

it concludes with still more point,

> Consider Phlebas, who was once handsome and tall as you.

Hence this part closes, after the fashion of others, by including the
audience in its frame of reference.

But if the ultimate fate of the protagonist has been indicated, neither
his fortune as told by the Madame, nor his experience in the Hyacinth
garden, has been exhausted. Hence what remains must belong to a
different order of experience from that which properly terminates in
death by water, or else to a different attitude toward water.

V

After 'Death by Water', representing the fate of his card, the agony of
the protagonist is intensified, and he turns from the water that drowns
to the water that saves—to the search for another river, associated with
the origin of the Tarot cards. Now the gardens and agony of Part I
merge into the trials of Christ or the Hanged God, and unite them in
the conclusion that he is dead and we are dying. Now 'the agony in
stony places' and its fear are intensified both by thirst for water and
doubt of its existence. The search of Part V—for its parts make one
journey—leads ultimately to the sacred river and its wisdom. Throughout, the illusionary character of the protagonist's vision increases as
his fortune converges.

The experience of agony and its doubt rise out of the physical conditions of this journey through the Waste Land, the desert scene of Part
I, which emphasizes the need of water. After observing, 'here is no

water but only rock', the spirit is tortured by the desire of water and no rock, or rock and also water, or merely the sound of water, even the illusion of its sound; 'but there is no water'. This torment has developed, by thematic imagery, from the 'red rock' through the 'Lady of the Rocks' to 'only rock'.

Physical and spiritual anguish distort his vision as he walks with the last shadow of his fortune, the Fisher King, once guardian of the Grail. Beside this unnamed figure he sees another, 'gliding wrapt in a brown mantle, hooded'; it is the Hanged Man or Christ. But again uncertainty besets him, for he cannot identify the figure. The notes prepare us for 'the journey to Emmaus', and this helps to confirm the identity of Christ but adds nothing to the essential experience. This, too, is a journey made by the 'slow of heart to believe all that the prophets have spoken' (Luke 24), including resurrection; but none of the notes really adds to the realization of its agony.

Likewise, as the vision continues, 'the present decay of eastern Europe' is realized quite apart from any need to identify it by a note. It organizes the chaos of the Waste Land, out of earlier materials in the poem, into an unreal image that turns them inside out and upside down. There is 'maternal lamentation', as for the dead god; but the 'hooded hordes' have their hoods because of their inability to see the 'hooded' one. Here we find the 'crowds of people, walking round in a ring'—the last item mentioned by Madame Sosostris; they already simulate the motions of Phlebas 'entering the whirlpool'. Now the unreal city extends to the east, embracing centres of various cultures; the 'lady of situations' fiddles lullabies on her hair to 'bats with baby faces', adding frustration to maternal lamentation; the bells, towers, and chanting voices of 'The Fire Sermon' are all inverted; the 'empty cisterns and exhausted wells' dry up the fountain and cistern of the Ecclesiastes passage echoed in Part I, where the poem centres on the 'dust' image.

After the vision of the disintegrating city, the protagonist draws near the chapel 'in this decayed hole among the mountains'; the reader should recall the mountains of Part I. The chapel, the note tells us, is more than a chapel; it is the Perilous Chapel of the Grail legend, and the Perilous Cemetery is also suggested. But they have lost their terrors, and hence their meaning. The spirit's abode is in ruins, 'only the wind's home', and its 'dry bones can harm no one'; it belongs to 'rats' alley'. Here we should recall the opening of Part III: 'the wind Crosses the brown land, unheard'. The quester denies their former meaning; and then, as with Peter, the cock crows, but as if in a French nursery rhyme. It is another use of the bird sounds that are so significant in the poem, and also of the irony of the naïve. But only a weathercock stood on the rooftree in a flash of lightning—yet it is a legendary portent. If this is the storm of the legend, the weathercock on the wind's home serves to point its direction, even to herald the 'damp gust bringing rain'. In terms of the nature symbolism (vegetation myth) it answers the doubt and denial: there is water, announced in a flash of lightning.

And Ganga (the Ganges) in the Waste Land waits for it. The sacred river, now sunken, was the home of the earliest vegetation myths, and its religious thought is represented here by words from an Upanishad, which is identified in the notes. Then we hear the 'reverberation of thunder of spring over distant mountains', which these words interpret. They are the conditions of the promise of spring which answers the doubt and denial expressed in this quest for the water of life.

The onomatopoetic voice of the Thunder is not left untranslated in the poem, for each command is suggested by the response. The question supplies 'give' and the answer follows. Their giving has been a surrender to passion, not love—as the poem abundantly illustrates. Yet, while self-regarding, this is their only evidence of life or existence; but it is not found in their obituaries, epitaphs ('memories'), or wills.

The second command is less clearly suggested, but it again is opposite to their reality. The prison of self or pride in which each is locked prevents their sharing the concern of others. Sympathy is the key that would unlock this prison, but each is certain of his isolation only at nightfall, when his world seems to close in around him. At best tenuous rumours reach and give respite to the proud Coriolanus in exile. The note quotes a philosophical basis for this isolation of the self, which frustrates the potentiality even of their kind of giving.

The reply to the third command clearly indicates 'control', or response to control. This response of the heart counters the surrender to blood and is presented in imagery appropriate to the Sailor and Part IV. It extends that moral from the fate of the Sailor to an image of the heart glad in obedience to the will, from its 'blood shaking' to 'beating obedient'. This completes the conditions of ascent to the higher love which might develop out of their experience, including that of the protagonist, and which would relieve their anguish.[4] These commands have all been violated in the Waste Land.

If this is the visionary journey which the protagonist takes in search of the water of life, it leaves him sitting upon the shore, with the arid plain rather than the unreal city behind him. Once more fishing, his final guise is that of the Fisher King, to whose line he belongs; but without regeneration his fate is as hopeless as that of the Sailor. Having travelled the Grail road to no avail, he ends in the knowing but helpless state of the Fisher King. Now that the Thunder has spoken, he is the Man with Three Staves—with three cardinal virtues that could be supports, that would ensure the rain. But awareness is not will, and so he thinks of preparing for death, with a question that recalls Isaiah (38:1): 'Set thine house in order: for thou shalt die, and not live.' This preparation involves some account of his fishing for life, of the fragments of 'broken images' which he has shored against his ruins.

These define not only his predicament and state of mind, but the discoveries that are indicated in the poem. As partial quotations they

[4] See 'Dante', *Selected Essays*, pp. 234–5.

are in fact 'fragments' that have their full meaning in other contexts; they summarize the 'broken images' of truth left in the Waste Land. Even nursery rhymes may contain or hide terrible truths; so 'London Bridge' presents an image of modern disintegration. And these fragments follow: 'Then he hid him in the fire which refines them . . . when shall I be as the swallow—O swallow swallow . . . the Prince of Acquitaine at the ruined tower'. This is the state of mind that attends the approaching 'wrack' of Ferdinand. If the tower points to his ruins, there may be a saving ambiguity in 'against'—against ultimate ruin. These fragments are all identified in the notes, but they speak for themselves; however, their connections require some comment. The first—from the Arnaut Daniel passage again—presents an image of voluntary suffering for purgation, the purgatorial burning hinted at the end of Part III; the second expresses the desire for regeneration, and connects with the nightingale image of 'inviolable voice': the third, to which the swallow's attention seems to be implored, presents an image of the protagonist's predicament, suggesting both the tower of self and the ruined chapel. Thus, even in their broken state, these fragments form a pattern.

Then the protagonist turns on the reader, as he turned at the close of Part I, and declares, in words of *The Spanish Tragedy* (IV, i), 'Why then Ile fit you'—that is supply you with what is suitable. And the irony is capped, while the seriousness is hidden, by the addition, 'Hieronymo's mad againe'. We may recall that the 'show' Hieronymo promised was to be his revenge; that he could supply it because he had given his youth to 'fruitless poetry'; and that its parts were originally in 'sundry Languages'. If these fragments substitute for the show, their ironic overtones may echo through these associations—even if the author has not thought it good, or possible, to set them down in English, 'more largely, for the easier understanding to every public reader'. Now the repetition of the Sanskrit commands, supported by the Upanishad ending, sounds like the mad talk of Hieronymo, and hallucinative vision appears to end in madness.

If this account of the poem seems to minimize the anthropological framework, it is for a very special reason. The framework is a means rather than an end, for the end is concerned with both the development and the decline of religious feeling in modern man. It is true that the anthropology reflects this development in the history of the race, but this reflection lends weight rather than direction to the poem. Neither is its direction taken from the idea that 'where the anthropological outlook prevails, sanctions wither'. While the emotional significance of the poem at no point is independent of this framework, it is likewise not equivalent to the framework, even when it seems most congruent.

From *Modern Philology*, Vol. 47, No. 1, 1949, pp. 197–206.

AUDREY F. CAHILL

The Hollow Men

In contrast to 'The Waste Land', 'The Hollow Men' is simpler in structure and conception. 'The Waste Land' represents universal chaos by revealing a series of insights into individual lives expressive of that chaos; its structure is episodic, and its effect depends greatly on the cumulative effect of the episodes. What the parts add up to is an overwhelming impression of mankind in retreat from meaning. The 'heap of broken images' is indeed terrifying, not simply because the images are broken, but because they are so many. While the same situation is presupposed in 'The Hollow Men', it is only presupposed, and not presented in detail; and the poem is a lyrical and symbolic comment on that situation. Its process is a simplifying, intensifying one in which, in spite of some difficulties of detail, the main issue is made clear.

The predicament of the hollow men is that of the Waste-Landers: they lack the 'courage to be'[1] and they have lost their reality because they have never affirmed it. They are remembered

> not as lost
> Violent souls, but only
> As the hollow men,
> The stuffed men.
>   (p. 87)[2]

In his essay on Baudelaire, Eliot writes,

> it is better, in a paradoxical way, to do evil than to do nothing: at least, we exist.[3]

The hollow men are those who have not even existed to the extent of doing evil. Their malady lies not in any civil intention, but in their evasion of any intention whatever.

. . . The hollowness of the hollow men is explored in several of the recurring symbols which appear in the poem. Though some of the images work by evocative suggestion rather than by definite denotation, there are a few symbols which seem to be used with a great measure of consistency, and which give a clue to the meaning of the more difficult passages.

---

[1] Cf. Paul Tillich, *The Courage to Be.*
[2] Page references are to Eliot's *Collected Poems 1909–1935.*
[3] *Selected Essays*, p. 429.

One of the symbols which emphasize the evasiveness of the hollow men is that of the eyes. While it is not clear whose eyes they are, it is enough that they represent spiritual challenge, and that the hollow men's refusal to meet them represents evasion of spiritual challenge. The eyes appear first as

> Eyes I dare not meet in dreams;
> > (p. 87)

and the shrinking from

> > that final meeting
> In the twilight kingdom
> > (p. 88)

suggests that they may be Christ's own, which

> Those who have crossed
> With direct eyes, to death's other Kingdom
> > (p. 87)

have presumably not evaded. The eyes are noticeably absent from the twilight world in which the hollow men exist:

> The eyes are not here
> There are no eyes here
> In this valley of dying stars.
> > (p. 89)

In the fourth poem the eyes are linked with the perpetual star, and their appearance (which is suggested only as a possibility) evokes hope as well as fear;

> The hope only
> Of empty men.

This confirms their significance as a symbol of divine demand, and suggests that perhaps Maxwell is right when he links them with Dante's vision of the Blessed Virgin in Paradise.[4]

Another obvious symbol is the guy referred to in the epigraph and providing the terms of the description of the hollow men in the first section of the poem. It is a significant caricature of humanity without a purpose: its human shape mocks human powerlessness, while its apparent mimicry of human gesture ridicules the futility of human communication that is without meaning:

> Shape without form, shade without colour,
> Paralysed force, gesture without motion.
> > (p. 87)

Associated with the image of the guy, and fulfilling a similar function, is the scarecrow suggested in the lines

[4] D. E. S. Maxwell, *The Poetry of T. S. Eliot*, p. 139. See below, p. 48.

Let me also wear
Such deliberate disguises
Rat's coat, crowskin, crossed staves
In a field
Behaving as the wind behaves.
         (p. 88)

This too, seems to be mocking human behaviour and it is this guise that
the hollow men choose to assume. They do not want to assert their
freedom in any spiritual or moral choice; they chose rather to act
arbitrarily, gratifying their most immediate needs, but being guided by
no transcending purpose.

A third symbol which recurs several times in the poem is that of the
two contrasting kingdoms. Both are kingdoms of death: the contrast
lies in the fact that the kingdom of this world is more shadowy and less
real than the kingdom beyond the grave. Like the world perceived by
Sweeney in 'Fragment of an Agon',

Death or life or life or death
Death is life and life is death.
         (p. 131)

It is helpful for the understanding of the poem to assume that, in the
poem 'death's dream kingdom' always means this world, as distinct
from 'death's other kingdom', the place of

Those who have crossed
With direct eyes.

This consistency about the recurring key symbols is characteristic of
Eliot's poetry: the music in 'Portrait of a Lady' and the water in 'The
Waste Land' do not alter in their fundamental meaning, although the
importance of that meaning is determined by the context in which they
appear. I do not think it unreasonable to expect the same measure of
consistency in the symbol of the two kingdoms, the significance of which
is perhaps most clear in the short poem 'Eyes that last I saw in tears'
(p. 143), which appeared first in the *Criterion* of January 1925, with
Parts II and IV of 'The Hollow Men'. In this poem, the poet is

Here in death's dream kingdom.[5]

considering the possibility of another meeting

At the door of death's other kingdom.

In 'The Hollow Men', 'death's dream kingdom' is a place of evasion:

The eyes are not here
There are no eyes here,
         (p. 89)

[5] My italics.

while in 'death's other kingdom', the dead remember the hollow men
—or forget them. This is an inversion of the idea that the dead 'live on'
in the memory of the living. Here, the lives of the living are so unreal
that they exist, if at all, only in the memory of those who, though dead,
are more real than they.

The world of the hollow men is described also as 'dead land', 'cactus
land', 'this broken jaw of our lost kingdoms'. Like the Waste Land, it
is a region where nothing is fruitful, for the human endeavour of the
hollow men is barren. In this desert environment, desire is misdirected
and frustrated and passionate need meets with no response:

> Is it like this
> In death's other kingdom
> Waking alone
> At the hour when we are
> Trembling with tenderness
> Lips that would kiss
> Form prayers to broken stone.
>   (pp. 88–9)

Worship, too, is misdirected: the stone images are as dead as the men
who worship them, and relationship with any god is as meaningless for
the hollow men as their attempts at relationship with any human being.

The star-image is another key image in the poem. In the lines

> More distant and more solemn
> Than a fading star
>   (p. 88)

it seems to be used primarily for its evocativeness, but in other passages
it is more clearly a symbol. In the third section,

> Under the twinkle of a fading star

seems to refer to some spiritual reality, or a consciousness of some
spiritual reality, which is disappearing. It seems to associate the star of
Bethlehem with the travellers' guiding star, and it hints also at the idea
that the sun is in fact a fading star which will one day cease to give
sufficient heat for the subsistence of life on earth. Thus the image
conveys a sense of the loss both of spiritual guidance and of sustaining
life. The powers that make possible human life, and indeed any life at
all, are vanishing, leaving humanity

> In this valley of dying stars,

where

> We grope together
> And avoid speech
> Gathered on this beach of the tumid river.
>   (p. 89)

In the fourth section the star and the eyes are linked, and become more definitely symbols of grace, which will give hope and sight to empty men. The eyes are no longer challenging; the star is now 'perpetual', and both are equated with the

Multifoliate rose
Of death's twilight kingdom

which seems here to a be direct reference to Dante's image of the saints in Paradise, gathered in formation like the petals of a white rose:

In forma dunque di candida rosa
Mi si mostrava la milizia santa,
Che nel suo sangue Cristo fece sposa.

(In form, then, of a white rose displayed itself to me that sacred soldiery which in his blood Christ made his spouse.)[6]

As Dante bathes his eyes in the river of light and looks again at the celestial rose, the myriad saints enthroned there are seen to reflect in their eyes the light of God himself. This gives the rose the appearance of a vast shining circle, and I think it is this image that Eliot is using when he links the rose with the 'perpetual star'. If this is so, then the eyes in this passage become more definitely the eyes of saints, for it is the eyes which must reappear

As the perpetual star
Multifoliate rose

if there is to be any hope for the hollow men. D. E. S. Maxwell identifies the eyes as Mary's,[7] by reference to lines 39–41 of Canto XXXIII of the *Paradiso*:

Those eyes, of God beloved and venerated, fixed upon him who prayed, showed us how greatly devout prayers please her.

In view of their possible reappearance as the 'multifoliate rose' I think it more likely that the poet is thinking of myriad eyes together; but the difference does not affect the interpretation of the poem very much. It is immaterial whether the eyes, the star and the rose are intended as symbols of the Virgin herself (and all three have traditionally been used as such); or whether they signify the corporate body of the saints of whom Mary, in her capacity as the greatest and most highly venerated, is the obvious representative. In either case, it is through the saints, presumably through their prayers, that the hollow men may be given hope. But their salvation is only potential: they are doomed to remain

Sightless, unless
The eyes reappear
          (p. 89)

[6] *Paradiso*, XXXI, ll. 1–3.
[7] D. E. S. Maxwell, *The Poetry of T. S. Eliot*.

to give them a vision greater than their own, as the star will give them a light greater than their own. These are surely images of a grace dimly apprehended, but not grasped, and of the power of a God whose absence is felt with a poignancy that speaks of His reality. . . .

The tragedy of the hollow men is intensified because it is presented within the context of possible ultimate meaning: it gives the overall impression, not that life as a whole is meaningless, but that it has a purpose which the hollow men refuse to acknowledge, and is therefore meaningless for them. Even more than in 'The Waste Land' there is that sense of the potential greatness of humanity that gives significance to insignificance, and that reveals the spiritual chaos of the hollow men not so much in its relation to general spiritual chaos as in its relation to a possible, desirable order which they shrink from accepting. Perhaps 'The Hollow Men' communicates more immediately than 'The Waste Land' because it is less ambitious in form and therefore more easily grasped as a whole; but I think, too, that it has a greater unity and a closer organization which are a consequence of the poet's firmer conviction of the importance of that spiritual attitude which Tillich has called 'the courage to be'.

From Chapter 5 of *T. S. Eliot and the Human Predicament*, University of Natal Press, 1967, pp. 53–9.

Ash Wednesday

. . . The first poem of 'Ash Wednesday' begins with a line which is an almost literal translation of the first line of a poem of Cavalcanti's: 'Because I do not hope to turn again'. It is evidently not essential to make the connection with Cavalcanti: but the reader who does will find that it reinforces some of the suggestions of the English poem. Cavalcanti's adoration of the ideal figure of the Lady is part of the 'organization of sensibility' which is adopted in 'Ash Wednesday', and in this poem, written when he was dying in exile, his worship of the Lady is the only positive feeling, all else being exhaustion and despair. The line from Shakespeare's sonnet, 'Desiring this man's art and that man's scope' (Eliot has altered *art* to *gift*) is bound for most readers to carry some of its context with it:

> When, in disgrace with fortune and men's eyes,
> I all alone beweep my outcast state
> And trouble deaf heaven with my bootless cries,
> And look upon myself and curse my fate:
> Wishing me like to one more rich in hope. . . .

The themes of introspection, solitariness and despair are found in both poems quoted: and both are relevant to the first poem of 'Ash Wednesday', though the lines incorporated into Eliot's verse have so much taken on the colour of his own that they do not strike primarily as allusions. 'Mature poets steal'; the remark is well illustrated here.

The title under which the six poems now stand prepares us for poetry concerned mainly with the penitential side of the spiritual life: and the first poem deals with the processes of self-exploration and self-examination with which that begins. The movement of the first three stanzas is slow and grave. The repetition of 'because' gives the impression of 'la raison raisonnant'; the intellect is establishing the relations of things. 'Strive to strive' and 'know I shall not know' suggest the piercing through layer on layer of motive. 'I do not hope' is reiterated. In his preface to a translation of Pascal's *Pensées* Eliot speaks of a despair which was 'a necessary prelude to, and element in, the joy of faith'. This surely might be an account of the despair which is present in the first two verses of this poem.

The 'turn' in the first line establishes the pivot on which the whole work is to hang: in all those parts of the poem which deal with the labours of the reason and the will the turning movement is to recur. It is not to be defined as a turn from unrighteousness to righteousness, from the world to God, or from past to present: it is sometimes one and sometimes the other, and the ambiguity is fundamental. It is by the 'turn' that the two worlds between which the poem moves are kept present to our minds. 'Ash Wednesday' is a poem full of connections which are too subtle for the intellect, a poem which continually 'teases us out of thought'; but one need not go into it deeply in order to discover that the poem is full of suggestions of reverses and circlings, that in the whole there may be discerned a kind of spiral movement. . . .

The 'agèd eagle' in the first verse is a striking image: it has been complained of by one distinguished critic as a solemn and self-pitying description of a poet then in his early forties. Allen Tate and others have pointed out the irony of the expression and it can hardly be doubted that they are right. It is a mocking piece of self-characterization, a poet's ironic attack on the grandiose conceptions which poets sometimes entertain of themselves. The line from Shakespeare has already suggested that in this passage Eliot is concerned with poetic activity. Nothing could be more unlike Eliot than to call himself in all seriousness an agèd eagle, meaning thereby to suggest the grandeur and pathos of the poet's calling. In his essay on Baudelaire, which is contemporary with 'Ash Wednesday', Eliot mentions Baudelaire's poem 'L'Albatros'.

> Le Poète est semblable au prince des nueés
> Qui hante la tempête et se rit de l'archer.
> Exile sur le sol, au milieu des huées
> Ses ailes de géant l'empêchent de marcher.

'Ses ailes de géant' Eliot cites as an example of the 'romantic detritus' amongst Baudelaire's imagery. The poet as an agèd eagle, intended seriously, would surely fall under the same condemnation.

But there is another sense in which the agèd eagle may be taken. Allen Tate describes it as a secular image, but it is usually very much the opposite. Since the Psalmist wrote 'Thy youth shall be renewed as the eagle's' the image has been constantly used in religious contexts as one of spiritual regeneration; for the Middle Ages the rejuvenation of the agèd eagle was the symbol of Baptismal grace.[1] 'Why should the agèd eagle stretch his wings', although it primarily suggests a mocking statement of the apparent failure of poetic vigour, may well suggest also a reluctance to embark on the exacting process of spiritual rebirth. In

---

[1] A note on Dante's dream of the Eagle (*Purg.* ix) in the Temple Classics edition reminds one that in the Medieval Bestiaries the eagle is said to fly up in his old age into the circle of fire, where he burns off all his feathers and falls blinded into a fountain of water whence he issues with his youth renewed. Cf. *The Family Reunion*:

> And what of the terrified spirit
> Compelled to be reborn
> To rise toward the violent sun
> Wet wings into the rain cloud. . . .

this sense it is another instance of the stress on the pain of rebirth which haunts Eliot's poetry from 'April is the cruellest month' of 'The Waste Land' to 'I've been born and once is enough' (*Sweeney Agonistes*) and 'This birth was hard and bitter agony' ('Journey of the Magi').

It has often been said that the stress in Eliot's religious poetry is on the cost of the spiritual life. D. W. Harding says that 'the renunciation is more vividly communicated than the advance for which it is made'. I should not say that this is true of 'Ash Wednesday', however just it may be as applied to 'A Song for Simeon' or 'The Journey of the Magi'. The outstanding effect of 'Ash Wednesday' is one of movement—'the detail of the pattern is movement'—of progress and growth: precarious —'wavering between the profit and the loss' even in the last poem of the six—but still strong and living.

That there is a conflict is, of course, admitted: it is evident in the contradictory elements of

The infirm glory of the positive hour

and

The one veritable transitory power.

A quotation from Eliot's remarks on Baudelaire is perhaps relevant here. 'Either because he cannot adjust himself to the actual world he has to reject it in favour of Heaven or Hell: or because he has the perception of Heaven and Hell he rejects the present world: both ways of putting it are tenable.' The first stanza of 'Ash Wednesday' suggests the first hypothesis: the second stanza suggests the other. The last clause of the Lord's Prayer seems to be in the background of these verses: 'thine is the kingdom, the power, and the glory, for ever and ever': it is against this that the 'usual reign', the 'infirm glory' and the 'transitory power' are measured and seem to fall short.

Because I cannot drink
There, where trees flower, and springs flow, for
      there is nothing again.

The mirage recedes: the reality of which 'human kind cannot bear very much' prevails in the positive statements of the third stanza:

Because I know that time is always time
And place is always and only place
And what is actual is actual only for one time
And only for one place.

The 'I' is clearing away the processes of self-deception by which the actual conditions of human life are masked: the first step is the admission that 'time is always time'. The mind is now, to use a phrase from *Murder in the Cathedral*, 'whole in the present'. The rhythm, which has been halting except in lines which recall the unattainable, quickens and becomes resolute.

> I rejoice that things are as they are and
> I renounce the blessed face
> And renounce the voice.

The will comes into prominence in the joyful acceptance of things as they are. That it is a *blessèd* face which is renounced is at first surprising. A Dante-Beatrice relationship is suggested in much of 'Ash Wednesday': and Dante's apprehension of God was *through* Beatrice. But Dante's 'first light' had to end with Beatrice's death and the enunciation here may be of the physical presence of a beloved woman. Or possibly it may be that courtesy of the spirit which accepts the absence of spiritual consolations without complaint, and is content to wait in stillness.

In the next line the stress falls naturally on the word *cannot*: 'Because I cannot hope to turn again'. It is as if the conflict is ended, one party having sustained defeat.

> Consequently I rejoice, having to construct something
> Upon which to rejoice.

The paradox is evident. The poem itself may well be the construction 'upon which to rejoice'. . . .

In the last two stanzas the poem approaches the verge of prayer: the need for mercy is recognized, and judgment deprecated: there is an effort to dismiss the recollection of the past and to quiet the activity of the mind. The tone is grave and there is complete simplicity. In the last verse the wings which are

> no longer wings to fly
> But merely vans to beat the air

are in one sense suggestive of impotence and melancholy: as if the self sees that from the point of view of the natural man it is decayed from its original vigour: but 'vans beating the air' may also suggest the winnowing movement which separates corn from chaff. The wings are serving a purpose, making the air thoroughly small and dry, so that the will, the instrument of prayer, may take over. There is focusing of attention,

> Teach us to care and not to care

and the long stream of mediation comes to an end in the stillness of prayer.

The language of the last two lines is no longer the poet's own: the 'I' is lost in the voice of the Church invoking Mary. The repetition of 'now and at the hour of our death' stresses the relation of the present to eternity. Life is felt as

> The time of tension between birth and dying

in the first poem as well as in the sixth.

It seems that the second poem of 'Ash Wednesday', originall
'Salutation I', was the first in order of composition. In its original forn
an epigraph *e vo significando* related it to a passage in the *Purgatorio* i
which Bonagiunta da Lucca, a poet of the older fashion, recognizes i
Dante the new poet of the sweet new style. 'I am one who when lov
inspires find melody and as he dictates to my mind, so do I giv
utterance.' Of the six poems which make up 'Ash Wednesday' this i
the one which most strikingly shows Eliot's *stil nuovo*. It is unlik
anything that he had written before and perhaps unlike anything els
that has been written in English, in its cadences and in its suggestions
Beneath the clarity and animation of its surface are themes which ar
the staple of Catholic Christianity: the renewing power of grace, th
vicarious life of the Church, the doctrine of the Communion of Saint:
The form is definite, objective and impersonal. The poem might we:
be an expression of that 'higher dream' whose disappearance Elic
regrets in his book on Dante. It has pre-eminently the air of somethin
'given': there is a miraculous ease and lightness about the rhythms an
about the experience which they communicate. In itself a complet
and rounded poem, in relation to the other parts of the sequence thi
vision is one of the 'hints and guesses, hints followed by guesses' whic
are spoken of in 'The Dry Salvages'. The first poem showed the strug
gles of the individual and the labours of the reason and the will: in th
second grace is at work and everything is easy.

> As I am forgotten
> And would be forgotten, so I would forget
> Thus devoted, concentrated in purpose.

There is no wavering between the profit and the loss here:

> We are glad to be scattered, we did little good to each other.

The subject of the vision is death: not the death of the body but
spiritual dissolution, a dying to self, which from the spiritual point (
view (and here no other is relevant) is seen as wholly gain. It is evide:
that the elements of the dream come partly from Dante and partly fro:
the Scriptures, in particular from the later chapters of Ezekiel. Through
out the sequence Eliot adopts Dante's 'organization of sensibility—th
contrast between higher and lower carnal love, the transition fro:
Beatrice living to Beatrice dead, rising to the cult of the Virgin'. Th
Lady who is saluted is a figure who in relation to the 'I' of the poem
something of what Lucia, Matelda and, supremely, Beatrice are to th
Dante of the *Purgatorio*, a Lady who 'helps him on his way': it is

> Because of the goodness of this Lady
> And because of her loveliness and because
> She honours the Virgin in meditation

that the bones 'shine with brightness'. The 'Because . . . and becaus
echo the 'Because I do not hope' of the first poem, but a different log

obtains here. And as what Beatrice is for Dante, Mary is, in a sense, for all; so that at a given point in the *Purgatorio* critics are not sure whether it is Mary or Beatrice who is spoken of: either may be 'the lady who above, acquires grace for us'; so the Lady who 'is withdrawn in a white gown, to contemplation', the 'Lady of Silences', is invoked in lines which recall some of the Virgin's titles.

Dante's spotted leopard is a gay but sinister beast: the three white leopards here are, on the contrary, agents of good, and Matthiessen is surely right in rejecting the suggestion that they personify the World, the Flesh and the Devil. They are more likely to be the goodness of the Lady, her loveliness, and the fact that she honours the Virgin in meditation.

The whiteness and the brightness of the bones are lovely. The dissembling of the 'I' is not conceived of as an outrage: whatever may be the similarities of technique the mood of the scene is in complete contrast to that evoked by the destruction of the body in Baudelaire's 'Voyage au Cythére'. The gruesomeness of some of the details—'my legs my heart my liver and that which had been contained in the hollow round of my skull and the indigestible portions which the leopards reject'—is nearer to being playful than horrific. One may find in this part of the poem something of that 'alliance of levity and seriousness, by which the seriousness is intensified', of that 'toughness which may be confused with cynicism by the tender-minded', which Eliot attributes to Marvell. There is no hint of pathos. The 'I' co-operates in the work of dissolution:

> I who am here dissembled
> Proffer my deeds to oblivion, and my love
> To the posterity of the desert and the fruits of the gourd.

There is enough of him left to see and record the scene—

> It is this which recovers
> My guts, the strings of my eyes and the indigestible portions
> Which the leopards reject.

Perhaps this is a hint that there must always be a residuum of self in a poet, without which there would be no need to write poetry. It is not necessary to account for the setting by a quotation from St John of the Cross, 'an immense desert . . . the more delectable, pleasant and lovely for its secrecy, vastness and solitude', although this may be relevant to the spiritual state which is being described. It is certainly a 'delectable' desert, without heat or thirst: the sand is a 'blessing', the day 'cool'. The paradox of the garden in the desert and the rose in the desert are to be found in Isaiah. The juniper-tree recalls that under which Elijah despaired: 'he requested for himself that he might die. And as he lay and slept under the juniper-tree, behold, then an angel touched him and said unto him, "Arise and eat".' The bones in the desert and the prophesying to the wind come from Ezekiel's vision of the regeneration

E

of Israel—a passage connected in the liturgy with the spiritual regeneration of baptism. 'Our bones are dried and our hope is lost.'

It is a kind of litany, not of supplication but of rejoicing, which the
bones sing, 'chirping' to the Lady of Silences 'with the burden of the
grasshopper'. The phrase here surely has none of the melancholy
associations of its original context, in Ecclesiastes; there is faintness
perhaps and feebleness, but it is difficult for 'chirping' to have anything
but a cheerful sound. As has been said the 'Lady of Silences' at first
suggests the Lady who is engaged in contemplation: but the paradoxical
attributes in the subsequent lines suggest a more transcendent figure,
the Virgin herself or the Church. 'Rosa Mystica' is one of Mary's
titles. In the *Paradiso* she is that 'Rose in which the Word Divine made
itself flesh'. 'Terminate torment of love unsatisfied' and 'End of the
endless journey to no end' seem to derive from St Bernard's hymn to
the Virgin in *Paradiso* XXX in which she is called 'Termine fisso
d'eterno consiglio'. . . .

In the earlier version the lines

> Rose of Memory
> Rose of Forgetfulness

were echoed by two other lines, now deleted, after the phrase 'Grace to
the Mother':

> For the end of remembering
> End of forgetting. . . .

The stress on memory and forgetfulness, both conceived as benefits,
recalls the streams of Lethe and Eunoe which run through Dante's
Earthly Paradise or Garden of Eden. 'On this side it (the water)
descends with a virtue which takes from men the memory of sin: on the
other it restores the memory of every good deed.' In the first part of
'Ash Wednesday' the poet prays that he may forget

> These matters that with myself I too much discuss
> Too much explain.

In the second the prayer is answered.

The paradox of 'the Garden where all loves end' and of 'the Garden
where all love ends' is not to be limited to one interpretation: but the
obvious sense is that while the lower loves come to an end here, in the
sense of being concluded, the higher love here reaches its destination,
its consummation.

After the Litany the poem returns to the firm, light, dancing
rhythms of the opening:

> Under a juniper-tree the bones sang, scattered and shining
> We are glad to be scattered, we did little good to each other.

The bones seem no longer to represent a single person, but many
having undergone the same transmutation,

Forgetting themselves and each other, united
In the quiet of the desert.

Personalities are sunk in the communion of saints, intent on a common
object of worship; that is not the whole meaning of the passage but it
is perhaps part of it.

The concluding lines of the poem quote Ezekiel's description of the
dividing of the land, which occurs after the vision of the building of the
Temple and the healing of the waters: 'This is the land which ye shall
divide by lot unto the tribes of Israel for inheritance: and these are
their portions, saith the Lord God.'

> This is the land which ye
> Shall divide by lot. And neither division nor unity
> Matters. This is the land. We have our inheritance.

The bones are as little careful of their own rights or envious of those of
others as the blessed in Dante's *Paradiso*. The second poem ends on a
note of absolute assurance and content. . . .

The vision of the desert and the Lady is over: it may have helped the
'I' of the poem on his way as the first of Dante's three dreams advanced
him to the entrance of Purgatory: but, the dream ended, Dante has to
climb the steps into Purgatory unaided, and the third poem of 'Ash
Wednesday' returns, as the opening lines suggest, to the labours of the
will. The struggle is resumed: the 'I' who did not hope to turn, turns
again and again as he mounts the stair: the struggle is now with the evil
whose presence is felt in the 'devil of the stairs' and the 'fetid air'. Evil
is represented here, as it is in *Murder in the Cathedral*, by images
repugnant to sense and touch. Eliot's stair is his own version of the
usual image of spiritual progress: it is not pure symbol; it exists in its
own right, too, with its banister, its damp, dark step, its window on to
the meadow. . . .

The springtime scene perceived through the voluptuously shaped
window of the third stair is lovely, but with a nostalgic loveliness, en-
chanting and relaxing, which is in complete contrast to that of the life-
giving, paradisal spring of the next poem. The scene and the music are
not sinister in themselves, but they distract the mind from the ascent of
the staircase. In *Murder in the Cathedral* imagery which has some
resemblance to that of the 'pasture scene' is used to represent the
'natural vigour in the venial sin'. The first and least formidable of the
tempters reminds the Archbishop of 'Fluting in the meadows': and
Thomas remembers, 'Not worth forgetting'.

The third stair itself is not described. The ascent of it is not achieved
unaided and its climax is a movement of humility. The words of the
centurion are associated by the Church with the rite of Holy Communion and it is perhaps that which is 'Ash Wednesday's' equivalent of
the Purgatorial healing, or the step of red porphyry. 'Speak the word
only and thy servant shall be healed.'

The Fourth poem returns to the 'higher dream'. There is much of Dante here. The 'eternal dolour' and the appeal of Arnaut recall Dante verbally, and the whole scene is related to that in which Dante meets a Beatrice 'risen from flesh to spirit', in the Earthly Paradise. The scene is precise in detail but vague in outline: 'who walked' may refer to a single figure or to several, according to the interpretation given to 'Who moved among the others as they walked': the one who wears white light may or may not be the same as the 'silent sister'. The first lines

> Who walked between the violet and the violet
> Who walked between
> The various ranks of varied green

may suggest a figure threading its way through the paths of a garden: but the violet and the green are not committed to being flowers or leaves: they may be taken as liturgical colours, or as formal order, or carefulness, discipline, 'concentration of purpose'. The colours used in this poem are all capable of symbolical meanings: the violet of penance, the green of hope, the white of purity, the blue of celestial things; but it is 'blue of larkspur' as well as 'of Mary's colour'. Surface appearances here are not merely to be transcended, although of course they suggest meanings which transcend them. Thus 'larkspur' too may have ethereal suggestions as in Hopkins' poems on St Dorothea.

The nunlike figure through whom the scene is evoked is not described: the stages of her progress are stressed—she 'moved among the others', 'talking of trivial things', before she 'made strong the fountains'—a renewing of the sources of life for others which recalls the activity of contemplation to which the Lady of the second poem withdrew. There is a contrast between the simplicity and ordinariness of her behaviour, and her achievement in the spiritual realm: between her ignorance and her knowledge. 'Eternal dolour' at first suggests the pains of Hell,

> Per me si va nell' eterno dolore,

but the dolour may be that of the Passion. There is no 'I' in this poem: but the 'sovegna vos' of Arnaut relates the figure in white and blue to a penitent who asks for her prayers.

It was in the Divine Pageant that Dante saw the glorified Beatrice and felt the tokens of the ancient flame. After a break in this poem the years move in a sort of procession,

> bearing
> Away the fiddles and the flutes, restoring
> One who moves in the time between sleep and waking, wearing
> White light folded, sheathed about her.

The 'white light' and the 'bright cloud of tears' are Eliot's version of that 'imagery of light' by which, as he says, Dante conveys the notion of beatitude. Dante several times describes figures swathed ('fasciato') in light or joy, and 'swathed' has perhaps suggested both the purely pictorial 'folded' and the 'sheathed' which adds suggestions of the flower and the sword. It is not only the figure of a lost love which is given back:

The new years walk, restoring
With a new verse the ancient rhyme.

The poetic power which in the first poem seemed to be felt as declining is rejuvenated. 'Restoring the years' modulates into 'Redeeming the time', the urgent cry that echoes through 'Burnt Norton':

Redeem
The unread vision in the higher dream
While jewelled unicorns draw by the gilded hearse.

The mysterious effect is surely intended: it is perhaps part of the 'unread vision'. The unicorn is in place in the medieval and formal setting of this poem (one finds it, for instance, in Cavalcanti), and the whole line continues the effect of the procession of pageant, conjuring up a picture like those Florentine engravings which illustrate Petrarch's Triumphs. It is in the Triumph of Chastity that the car drawn by unicorns appears: what is suggested here is rather the apparent Triumph of Time.

The figure in white and blue who 'talked of trivial things' is now the 'silent sister'. The garden god is here too, but his flute is 'breathless', impotent to enchant and distract. It is the silence of the sister which is powerful and when she 'signs', perhaps making the sign of the Cross, the garden springs into fresh life. The yews which frame the nun-like figure are symbols which occur several times in Eliot's poetry from 'Animula' onwards—'Pray for Floret by the boar-hound slain between the yew-trees'. If they have a literary ancestry I am ignorant of it. But the yews' suggestions of mortality and immortality are not recondite. As the churchyard tree the yew must first suggest death: but it perhaps is the churchyard tree because its long life symbolizes immortality, and because it is, in Sir Thomas Browne's phrase 'an embleme of Resurrection from its perpetual verdure'.

The wind that is to 'shake a thousand whispers from the yew' must in the context suggest the spirit of God, as in the Canticles: 'Blow upon my garden that the spices thereof may flow out.' The line suggests a 'divine event'. But it is also merely the wind in the yew trees, with its own unfathomable meaning. There is a line in 'Anabase' which has something of the same sense of expectancy: 'I foretell you the time of a great blessing and the felicity of leaves in our dreams.'[2]

[2] Mr Raymond Preston in *Four Quartets Rehearsed* (Sheed and Ward, 1946) indicates an allusion in 'Ash Wednesday' to the bird in Grimm's fairy tale 'The Juniper Tree'. The tree in the poem is perhaps also to be connected with that in the fairy tale. When Marlinchen buried the little boy's bones beneath it the juniper 'began to stir itself—just as if someone was rejoicing and clapping his hands'. Marlinchen goes away 'as gay and happy as if her brother were still alive'.

The dream-scene makes death enviable and life an exile, as they appear in the 'Salve Regina', the invocation of Mary as Queen. It is with a phrase from this prayer that the poem ends: 'And after this our exile show unto us the blessed fruit of thy womb, Jesus.' On this undertone the poem moves to the mystery of the Logos.

In the fifth poem the scene widens from the intense experience of an individual soul, with its circlings between past and present, God and self, to the world whirling 'about the centre of the silent Word'. The 'I' who speaks here is not the worshipper but the Deity, using the Reproaches, the liturgical expression of Christ's griefs. 'O my people, what have I done unto thee, or wherein have I wearied thee? Testify against me. Because I brought thee forth from the land of Egypt thou hast prepared a cross for thy Saviour. . . .'

The rhythms with which the fifth poem opens are decided, intricate, almost declamatory, after the delicate and tentative music of Part IV: the first stanza leaves an impression of extreme mental activity and stress which is something like the effect of Andrewes' sermons, from which a phrase is borrowed. The play on 'word' and 'world' has caused the passage to remind one critic of Gertrude Stein's prose: but much of it is already present in the English version of the first chapter of St John's Gospel, the hymn to the Logos, on which the verse is based.

The Incarnation and the Passion are brought together: the silence of the Word is that of the speechless Babe and of the Christ who before his accusers 'opened not his mouth'. Silence as the condition of spiritual events has been stressed throughout 'Ash Wednesday': and many hints are now fulfilled—the 'speech without word and Word of no speech' of Part II; 'Speak the word only' of Part III; 'Spoke no word' of Part IV:

> Still is the unspoken word the Word unheard,
> The Word without a word, the Word within
> The world and for the world.

The second stanza explores the whole world for the right response to the Word.

> No place of grace for those who avoid the face
> No time to rejoice for those who walk among noise and deny the voice.

The face and the voice which were renounced in the first poem are here avoided and denied. The distinction is clear: to renounce is to refuse to make a claim; to avoid or deny is to refuse a claim that is made.

In the third and fourth verses there is a more personal note: the poet turns from surveying the world as a spectator to including himself in the number of those who, though they have responded, have not responded fully: and the rhythm becomes slower and quieter, lingering on the rhymes of the last line:

> Pray for those who chose and oppose.

The conflict is not only that which springs from the unresolvable tension between the material and the spiritual. The line

> torn on the horn between season and season . . . power and power

suggests also the strain imposed on those who are 'conscious, without remission, of a Christian and non-Christian alternative at moments of choice' (*Idea of a Christian Society*). The last verse enacts the struggle of man dealing with his own cowardice, conscious of the disparity between the outward allegiance and the inner betrayal. The imagery of the rocks and the desert presents a sequence of strenuous spiritual effort which seems to end in victory: 'Spitting from the mouth the withered apple-seed' may suggest the act of confession, the opening formula of which is quoted in the next poem: 'Bless me father, for I have sinned'. It may also, with a wider bearing, suggest that 'diminution of the traces of original sin' which Baudelaire saw as the essence of true civilization.

The last poem in many ways summons up the first. But the 'I' is not merely back at the point from which he started: it is now 'Although I do not hope' instead of 'Because'. While in the first poem the emphasis was on not hoping, not striving, here in spite of the assertions that life is a 'brief transit', 'a dream-crossed twilight', there are aspirations after natural vigour and unfettered movement: not

> Why should the agèd eagle stretch its wings?

but

> From the wide window towards the granite shore
> The white sails still fly seaward, seaward flying
> Unbroken wings.

Conflict continues, and it is perhaps a sharper conflict than in the first poem: but it is also more fully resolved. The sights and sounds and smells for which the lost heart quickens to rebel are fresh and bracing. They are in contrast to the seductive scene which was visible through the slotted window of the third poem. Of course they too are a distraction from the main purpose and are disavowed, as representing the natural man's desire to assert the reality known to the senses, to feel himself 'substantial flesh and blood'. They are dreams and false, dreams out of the ivory gates of Greek legend. But the longing for the sea is satisfied in that the landscape of the 'higher dream' opens upon the sea which is God's will. 'And his will is our peace: it is that sea to which all moves that it createth and that nature maketh' (*Paradiso*, III, 85). The spirit of the fountain and the garden is also the spirit of the river and the sea.

There is in the last poem none of the sense of painful constriction which a critic has discerned in the first, where the 'I' seemed to be enclosed in the cell of self-knowledge. There is spaciousness: the poet faces the sea. 'Even among these rocks' must suggest desolation, but the rocks derive from the sea: there is no hint of despair in the last poem, but a sense of complete dependence which issues in the final supplication:

Teach us to sit still
Even among these rocks
Our peace is His will
And even among these rocks
Sister, mother
And spirit of the river, spirit of the sea,
Suffer me not to be separated
And let my cry come unto Thee.

It is characteristic of the technique of 'Ash Wednesday' that the most poignant lines of the appeal:

Suffer me not to be separated
And let my cry come unto Thee

are not original expressions of religious feeling. 'Suffer me not to be separated from Thee' is a line from an ancient prayer, the 'Anima Christi', and the last line of all is part of the suffrages which the Church uses in many services: 'Lord, hear our prayer: and let our cry come unto Thee.'

'Ash Wednesday' is a poem of penance and preparation. By the time the end of the sequence is reached it is clear that there have been compensations for the face and voice which were renounced in the first part: but the face of the figure representing the new order of things is not seen, nor her voice heard: she is the 'silent sister veiled'. The end of 'Ash Wednesday' looks out on to the sea: it is in 'Marina' that 'the hope, the new ships' appear.

From *T. S. Eliot: A study of his Writings by Several Hands* edited by B. Rajan, Dennis Dobson Ltd, 1948, pp. 38–56.

The *Ariel* Poems

... 'Journey of the Magi' is the monologue of a man who has made his own choice, who has achieved belief in the Incarnation, but who is still part of that life which the Redeemer came to sweep away.[1] Like Gerontion, he cannot break loose from the past. Oppressed by a sense of death-in-life (Tiresias' anguish 'between two lives'), he is content to submit to 'another death' for his final deliverance from the world of old desires and gods, the world of 'the silken girls'. It is not that the Birth that is also Death has brought him hope of a new life, but that it has revealed to him the hopelessness of the previous life. He is resigned rather than joyous, absorbed in the negation of his former existence but not yet physically liberated from it. Whereas Gerontion is 'waiting for rain' in this life, and the hollow men desire the 'eyes' in the next life, the speaker here has put behind him both the life of the senses and the affirmative symbol of the Child; he has reached the state of desiring nothing. His negation is partly ignorant, for he does not understand in what way the Birth is a Death; he is not aware of the sacrifice. Instead, he himself has become the sacrifice; he has reached essentially, on a symbolic level true to his emotional, if not to his intellectual, life, the humble, negative stage that in a mystical progress would be prerequisite to union. Although in the literal circumstances his will cannot be fixed upon mystical experience, because of the time and condition of his existence, he corresponds symbolically to the seeker as described by St John of the Cross in *The Ascent of Mount Carmel*. Having first approached the affirmative symbol, or rather, for him, the affirmative reality, he has experienced failure; negation is his secondary option.

The quest of the Magi for the Christ child, a long arduous journey against the discouragements of nature and the hostility of man, to find at last a mystery impenetrable to human wisdom, was described by Eliot in strongly colloquial phrases adapted from one of Lancelot Andrewes' sermons of the Nativity:

A cold coming they had of it at this time of the year, just the worst time of the year to take a journey, and specially a long journey in. The ways deep, the weather sharp, the days short, the sun farthest off, *in solstitio brumali*, 'the very dead of winter'.[2]

[1] See Elizabeth Drew, *T. S. Eliot: the Design of his Poetry* pp. 118–19.
[2] Andrewes, *Works*, I, 257; *Selected Essays*, p. 297.

... The arrival of the Magi at the place of Nativity, whose symbolism has been anticipated by the fresh vegetation and the mill 'beating the darkness', is only a 'satisfactory' experience. The narrator has seen and yet he does not fully understand; he accepts the fact of Birth but is perplexed by its similarity to a Death, and to death which he has seen before:

> All this was a long time ago, I remember,
> And I would do it again, but set down
> This set down
> This: were we led all that way for
> Birth or Death?[3]

Were they led there for Birth or for Death? or, perhaps, for neither? or to make a choice between Birth and Death? And whose Birth or Death was it? their own, or Another's? Uncertainty leaves him mystified and unaroused to the full splendour of the strange epiphany. So he and his fellows have come back to their own Kingdoms, where,

> ... no longer at ease here, in the old dispensation,
> With an alien people clutching their gods

(which are now alien gods), they linger not yet free to receive 'the dispensation of the grace of God'.[4] The speaker has reached the end of one world, but despite his acceptance of the revelation as valid, he cannot gaze into a world beyond his own.

'A Song for Simeon' (1928) derived its title from the 'Nunc dimittis,' or 'Song of Simeon' in the Prayer Book. The prayer that follows the second lesson at Evensong is taken from chapter 2 of Luke, recounting the ritual presentation of the child Jesus at the temple. Eliot based his poem upon this passage. But in so doing he developed the character of Simeon into a parallel to that of the speaker in the previous monologue and, rather more conspicuously, to that of Gerontion. Simeon's spiritual crisis is not quite as in 'Journey of the Magi'; like Gerontion's it looks into the future. What Simeon sees is the harassment and persecution of those, ironically enough, who, like himself, shall credit the vision now appearing. Whereas Gerontion in his 'sleepy corner' sees destruction engulf the worldly or profane, Simeon, though awaiting a tranquil death for himself, sees the destruction, as the world accounts it, that must overtake the righteous. This is a necessary destruction if life is to come out of death, but Simeon himself is unprepared to face it. Here again is the renunciation of an old life without a concentrated search for 'the ultimate vision'. Simeon is not only a soul relinquishing the life of the senses, a Tiresias; he is a soul that through its greater prescience, as it were contagiously, bears the sufferings of men elected to encounter

---

[3] Cf. *Othello*, V, ii, 351: 'Set you down this.' See *Selected Essays*, p. 111.
[4] Eph. 3:2. This occurs in the Book of Common Prayer, Epistle for the Epiphany.

suffering through action. But in his own person he is not constrained to pass from the one realm into the other, from the old dispensation into the new. Thus like the Magi he is simply transient between two worlds; the difference is that like Tiresias he understands the movement from the one into the other. He has passed the stage of Gerontion, who has lost the Word, and that of the hollow men, who are not freed from the circuit of the prickly pear.

The monologue, a tired murmer of an old, old man, starts with a brief section displaying familiar symbols from 'Gerontion' and 'The Waste Land' to create a new statement concerning death and rebirth. The stubborn approach of spring, with hyacinths symbolizing pagan life and fertility, is contrasted with the stubborn duration of winter. Snow and flowers, as in 'Gerontion' and 'The Burial of the Dead', bring into opposition the two principles everlastingly alternating in the cycle, here again represented by an old man and a 'depraved May'. But the spring brings also the Child, and the hyacinths have a new meaning, in view of which the fertility cults of Rome belong with the 'winter sun' that 'creeps by the snow hills'. For in the spring a new Light shines, to turn pagan death into life, making an end of the old life, 'light . . . / Like a feather on the back of my hand'—recalling the final scene of *King Lear*. Meanwhile Simeon awaits 'the wind that chills towards the dead land', partly the whirlwind of death in 'Gerontion', partly the wind of the Spirit in Ezekiel, a breath restoring life to the dead through the death of Christ. The feather blown in the wind (contrast 'White feathers in the snow') will thus be blown into the hands of God.

But the change itself imposes a terrible trial upon the human soul. The surge of a new life, whether the sexual struggle of Gerontion and Tiresias or their spiritual struggle which is this narrator's as well, amounts to no placid awakening. Not for nothing is time's April 'the cruellest month'; it arouses the spirit to decision. The Women of Canterbury, in *Murder in the Cathedral,* beseech the Archbishop to return to France, that they may be spared the new suffering. Simeon, too, that he may not outlive this beginning, not participate in the vitalizing growth of the new faith, prays for peace through 'the still unspeaking and unspoken Word', the eternal countertype of strife. He resembles Gerontion or the protagonist of 'Journey of the Magi'; for he too is unwilling to be caught up in a life inflicting violence and calamity. In plea for a tranquil death, he offers testimony to his past righteousness:

I have walked many years in this city,
Kept faith and fast, provided for the poor,
Have given and taken honour and ease.
There went never any rejected from my door.

It is precisely 'honour and ease' that the future must withhold; his own 'faith and fast' will not avail in 'the time of sorrow'. Like Christ, 'despised and rejected of men; a man of sorrows, and acquainted with grief',[5] his posterity will be driven, Christian and Jew, 'to the goat's path, and the fox's home, / Fleeing from the foreign faces and the foreign swords'.[6] Christ himself is to say, 'The foxes have holes, and the birds of the air have nests; but the Son of man hath not where to lay his head.' The symbols here pertain to the Way of Sorrows and the Passion. Simeon is speaking of something which he cannot know about; what nevertheless assumes importance is not 'the mountain of Zion, which is desolate, the foxes walk upon it' (Lam. 5:18), but the scourging of Christ, the Stations of the Cross, the weeping of the Virgin on Calvary and even the day of the last 'abomination of desolation' when the inhabitants of Judea shall flee to the mountains. From such future vicissitudes, Simeon would be preserved through the peace of 'the still unspeaking and unspoken Word'.

This poem and 'Journey of the Magi' are in one way simpler and in another way more intricate than 'The Hollow Men'. First, they omit the harrowing struggle with sexual desire. They have, it is true, 'the silken girls' and the 'Roman hyacinths'; these, however, symbolize what the old men have already put away from them (the hyacinths, unlike those in 'The Waste Land', connoting little more than the pagan and sensual aspect of rebirth, like the lilacs bred 'out of the dead land') and no longer express the tension between lust and love that dismays Gerontion and Tiresias. Corresponding to the eyes of 'The Hollow Men' and the hyacinth girl of 'The Waste Land' are the Birth in 'Journey of the Magi' and the Word in 'A Song for Simeon'. These poems, like the others, set up an affirmative, numinous symbol, uniting flesh and spirit, and show it to be inapprehensible. The sufferers in them, as much as the hollow men, must turn unfulfilled toward death. The difficulty here is that a new element has obtruded into Eliot's usual pattern: the soul vanquished not by sex or unbelief but by sheer spiritual incapacity. The fact that these men are old, Eliot having economically used the same symbol of age to suggest impotence and unbelief (Gerontion) and twisted desire (Tiresias), seems to point to the Pauline sense of 'old man', the unregenerate. At any rate, the Magi and Simeon, like Gerontion, appear to symbolize the soul's enchainment to the past, and its inability to desert its bonds at the cost of a painful readjustment. These men are still in and of the world, still spiritually uncleansed of the human taint. It is this that makes them 'old' men: 'After such knowledge, what forgiveness?'

Though both of these poems depict the failure of affirmation, they do not explicitly praise the other way, of abnegation and martyrdom of spirit. But they draw up a pattern for *Murder in the Cathedral*, *The Family Reunion*, 'Four Quartets', and *The Cocktail Party*. The humility to which the Magi and Simeon descend is that of conscious ignorance and inadequacy. This humility, however, comes but a step before the

[5] Isa. 53:3.
[6] Cf. Conrad, 'Heart of Darkness', in *Youth*, p. 48: '. . . the foreign shores, the foreign faces'; cf. also Swinburne, 'Itylus'.

deliberately chosen ignorance of the mystical Dark Night as Eliot has described it in 'East Coker':

> In order to arrive at what you do not know
> You must go by a way which is the way of ignorance.

And that is the martyrdom of the 'old' man in soul and mind; it, in turn, comes but a step before the full sacrifice of Thomas Becket at Canterbury. Thus 'Journey of the Magi' and 'A Song for Simeon' are not entirely poems of despair. They foreshadow the way in which purgation compensates for the debility of body and will and the scars of disappointment.

Except for 'The Hollow Men', 'Animula' (1929) is Eliot's most pessimistic poem. The state described and its symbolic configuration are the same as in 'Journey of the Magi' and 'A Song for Simeon'.

> Wandering between two worlds, one dead,
> The other powerless to be born.

But those poems limit grief by pinpointing it in the dramatic contexts. They have a historical focus. Simeon and the Magi must endure an external necessity wherein they can know only the Incarnation, not the Atonement. It is not so much that their own potentialities are weak as that a superior order has confined them to a dispensation of law instead of love. The Atonement was retroactive without bestowing the consolation of perceived grace. These men have, but do not know, the benefits of Christ's still unrevealed sacrifice. They are joyless, and the more so because, Tantalus-like, they verge so close to what they cannot grasp. Curiously, in this one aspect, both poems are less, not more, intimate to the Eliot problem as such: detachment is mitigating. 'Animula', on the other hand, makes so general a pronouncement, not about a single spiritual dilemma but about the helplessness of the whole human condition, that it contrives to be more dismal and more personal at the same time. In 'Animula' the soul, despite its natural appetite for good, can do nothing whatever. By resistance and inertia, it misses an 'offered good' and ignores the grace extended.

As a philosophic poem, 'Animula' is prosaic in tone and traditional in metre. The rhyming pentameter is monotonously regular; the diction flat. One is dismayed to see in Eliot so cheap a phrase as 'fragrant brilliance' and to be afflicted with the unintended overtones of so carelessly chosen a name as 'Boudin'.[7] But the technical disorders of the poem do not infect the treatment of its theme.

As usual the discovery of hollowness in the world of the natural man heralds no spiritual rebirth. In 'Animula' the soul is kept back by the confused meshes of its past, by time, and can only live 'first in the silence

---

[7] Eliot perhaps picked up the name 'Boudin' from the Eumaeus episode of Joyce's *Ulysses*, p. 610, where it is appropriate as a sly allusion to Mr Bloom's appetite (as a common noun it generally means black pudding). Eliot overlooked this connotation.

after the viaticum'. The poem does not emphasize the desirability of
death and contains no hint of an overwhelming experience which as-
tonishes and arrests the eager soul in its progress. It suggests, however,
something of the immobile hopelessness depicted in Part V of 'The
Hollow Men', though, again, it lacks even the memory of any symbol
such as the eyes with their connotation of eternity coinciding with the
temporal world. The only analogue to the obsessive lost experience is a
gentle 'whisper of immortality',

> . . . pleasure
> In the brilliant fragrance of the Christmas tree,
> Pleasure in the wind, the sunlight and the sea.

In value this corresponds approximately to the pagan 'Roman hyacinths' of Simeon's past and to the 'regretted'

> . . . summer palaces on slopes, the terraces,
> And the silken girls bringing sherbet.

The new life toward which 'Animula' points is 'the warm reality, the
offered good, / . . . the importunity of the blood', just as in the preceding
poems the ideal is the Word and the Child. The inability to reach it is
identified both with the breaching of childhood naïveté and with the
invasion of this by adult perplexities, as in Vaughan's 'The Retreat' or
Wordsworth's 'Ode on Intimations of Immortality'.

> Full soon thy Soul shall have her earthly freight,
> And custom lie upon thee with a weight,
> Heavy as frost, and deep almost as life!

. . . Even though the soul takes its greatest pleasure in the search for
God, toward whom its free will, stimulated by appetite, naturally moves it,
is is easily deflected by frivolities and evils. 'Animula' assumes that such
distraction is inevitable. Blame for the soul's travail rests with the
'pain of living and the drug of dreams', from which ensue the cramping
of will, the inhibition and misdirection of desire. Stifled by all that
'perplexes and offends', the soul takes refuge in barren learning. It
becomes 'irresolute and selfish, misshapen, lame', no longer exuberant,
incapable of living. It seems to have no choice but denial, passivity. It
can yield to the behest neither of flesh nor of spirit.[8] . . .

'Marina' (1930) departs radically from the tone established in the
three poems grouped with it. Although its protagonist confronts a
symbol of vital restoration, the meeting signifies no transcendent

---

[8] Possible sources for the theme of 'Animula' include Baudelaire, 'Le Voyage'
(cited in *Selected Essays*, p. 249); Tennyson, 'In Memoriam', xlv; Cardinal
Newman, *The Idea of a University* (New York and London, 1927), pp. 331–32
(Preface to 'Elementary Studies'); and *The Education of Henry Adams*, p. 460.
The last has been noticed by Robert A. Hume, *Runaway Star : An Appreciation
of Henry Adams* (Ithaca, N.Y., 1951), p. 37.

communion impossible to him but, on a dream level, the benign and even triumphant realization of joy in a human relationship. The context designated in the title is that of Pericles' reunion with his daughter Marina in Shakespeare's *Pericles*. The recognition scene there (V, i) has more than once been extolled by Eliot for its dramatic and symbolic force.[9] The incredible, yet miraculously probable, reunion of the lost daughter with the old king in the drama is like a rebirth of the king himself, a recovery of hope despaired of. Marina's birth at sea— virtually, one might say, of the sea—is perfected by her deliverance from shame and death. To Pericles, finding her alive whom he has thought dead, she seems the incarnation of a vision.

Against this almost beatific discovery Eliot set for his epigraph line 1138 of Seneca's *Hercules Furens*, 'Quis hic locus, quae regio, quae mundi plaga?' ('What place is this, what land, what quarter of the globe?'). These words are the first clouded mutterings of Hercules as he awakes from the unconscious fit into which he has sunk overcome by madness. Having ascended from his labour in the underworld, where he secured the dog Cerberus, he has been driven to frenzy through Juno's jealousy of him as Alcmena's son. In his madness he has turned his envenomed arrows against his own children, and now, his senses gradually returning, he is about to recognize the enormity. The total situation, antithetical to that in *Pericles*, discloses, in contrast with the discovery of Marina in Eliot's poem, not only the horror of death but the horror of personal defeat suffered by Hercules. As the assassin of his children he has met disaster through a turn of Fortune's wheel, the reverse of that which has blessed Pericles; and whereas Pericles' daughter is alive, Hercules' children are lying slaughtered. The crime of Hercules succeeds a moment of overweening pride, the moment of his highest exultation; he has completed his twelfth and final labour and has killed the tyrant who abused his household, but he has incurred divine resentment. With such a career of arrogant boastfulness, leading to deprivation and ruin, Eliot contrasted the gracious experience of Pericles by a somewhat oversubtle mingling. In a letter written to Sir Michael Sadleir in May 1930, Eliot spoke of having used the scenes from the two plays so as to form a 'crisscross' between them. 'Marina' owes to Seneca the rhetoric of its opening line and the undercurrent of irony produced by the confluence of death and life.

The poem is a monologue, spoken precisely at the instant of recognition. Pericles is not sure whether he has crossed the boundaries of dream into reality. His experience belongs to a kind of halfway world, the atmosphere of which pervades his words. As in a dream, he is standing on the deck of a vessel approaching land, from whose granite shores are borne the scent of pine and the song of the woodthrush— images rising out of some buried recollection and made vivid as he becomes conscious of his daughter's presence. The images objectify the emotion stirring in him. They obliterate the memory of other images—

[9] See Drew, p. 127.

those of men associated with the sins of envy, pride, sloth, and con-
cupiscence, and with the state of death consequent upon habitual sin.
These

> Are become insubstantial, reduced by a wind,
> A breath of pine, and the woodsong fog
> By this grace dissolved in place.

Marina's apparent restoration has conferred a grace, a life-giving and
sin-purging benediction. His dreams seem palpable; Marina seems a
living creature in whom the idea, the figment, becomes objectively real
and in achieving transformation both clearer and less clear, because
different:

> What is this face, less clear and clearer
> The pulse in the arm, less strong and stronger—
> Given or lent? more distant than stars and nearer than the eye.[10]

She seems tangibly one who, as in 'Ash Wednesday', 'moves in the time
between sleep and waking':

> Whispers and small laughter between leaves and hurrying feet
> Under sleep, where all the waters meet.[11]

. . . Marina is not the Child from 'Journey of the Magi', but she is
invested, for purposes of the poem, with the characteristics of flesh
clothing a divine emanation. Thus at the instant of Pericles' recognition,
although (and because) it is not clear to him whether the child really is
'given', the images he associates with her are 'stars' and 'the eye'. These
are the same already adopted by Eliot in 'The Hollow Men'; again, they
are symbols, as are the leaves and the thrush, of the values inherent in
the Grail of the romances. Marina is the focal centre here, corresponding
in a purer form to the hyacinth girl of 'The Waste Land'. And for once
the communion is not abortive. The meeting brings together, at least
on one level of consciousness, a quester and the object of his quest, and
there is no division or disappointment.

Such beatitude is far from typical of Eliot's usual symbolic scheme.
But the happy nature of the experience in 'Marina' does not violate the
principle enunciated in his *After Strange Gods* (1934) that 'ideals' are
not the concern of poetry[12]—which can mean that poetry should not show

[10] Cf. *Pericles*, V, i, ll. 154–6:

> But are you flesh and blood?
> Have you a working pulse, and are no fairy?
> Motion?

[11] Cf. Sidney Lanier, 'The Marshes of Glynn,' ll. 101–3:

> . . . who will reveal to our waking ken
> The forms that swim and the shapes that creep
>   Under the waters of sleep?

[12] Eliot, *After Strange Gods*, p. 28.

unreal attainments as if they were true. Pericles' happiness occurs where the literal event is not actual and is not supposed to be actual, except as dream. The connection between the actuality of dream and that of waking is simply emotional; the experience has emotional authenticity....

Despite the differences between 'Marina' and the other 'Ariel Poems', it shares with them a quality looking back to the conclusion of 'The Waste Land' as well as to the spiritual struggle in 'Ash Wednesday'. The poem communicates its intuition that the obsolete desires and ambitions must be sloughed off before the soul can find its higher mode, its unequivocal unity with the vision. Thus 'Marina' is more Dantean and Platonic than its predecessors. It aspires to transcend the agony of the soul entangled in its past, voiced in earlier poems; it aspires also to transcend the frustration of the soul striving, as in 'Ash Wednesday', to be reconciled; and it reveals, without dwelling on the process of rebirth through suffering, the emotional state which rewards devotion, a state conferring tranquility and love. That this state is merely fore-shadowed is plain from the fact not only that 'Marina' unfolds as a dream landscape but also that Pericles articulates something like a prayer:

> . . . let me
> Resign my life for this life, my speech for that unspoken.

Since the poem has no past or future, one has perhaps no right to speculate on any for Pericles. But if one should imagine a future for him, it would have to be one in which he resigned the withered life for that heralded in his illuminative dream. Had Eliot not altered 'word' to 'speech' after his first draft, one might say something more about the creative and religious overtones of this line. What is crucial here is the possibility of putting the old life behind and moving upward, of 'faring forward', transhumanized, to 'the Garden / Where all love ends'.

From *T. S. Eliot's Poetry and Plays*, University of Chicago Press (enlarged edition 1960), pp. 122–34.

F

FRANK WILSON

The Musical Structure of the *Four Quartets*

We have it on the authority of Miss Helen Gardner that the 'Four Quartets' are constructed on a pattern similar to that of 'The Waste Land', and it is profitable to make some further examination of 'The Waste Land' in the light of these later poems. The musical framework of Eliot's symphony comes to seem rather like an enormous flying machine which the poet has constructed in order to negotiate heights of poetry otherwise unattainable for him. And I think Eliot found his contrivance rather unwieldy, and the compression and occasional distortion of statement which it necessitated not very satisfactory. It is not proven whether the 'Coriolan' is an unfinished second symphony, but I think it may be, and believe that the poet, when he wrote it, was trying to make his technique less noticeable to the reader. For 'The Waste Land' seems essentially the work of a young poet, taking pride in the exhibition of his technique even though he is at pains, in his notes, not to reveal its secret. When he wrote the 'Four Quartets', however, Eliot was more restrained. Here the technique, though it is still near that of the earlier poem, seems relatively unimportant: it is there to be unravelled, if the critic will, but as with the allegory of what I consider the most difficult poem in our language, it will not bite the critic, if he does not interfere with it. It may, however, be of use to examine the structure of the first of the 'Quartets', 'Burnt Norton', in its relation to that of the 'The Waste Land'.

The first movement of 'Burnt Norton' opens with a tentative and highly formal introductory passage, similar to that with which 'The Waste Land' begins, at least in so far as it prepares the reader not only for the movement, but for the whole body of the work it precedes. For the 'Quartets' are concerned in the first place with time, and what is stated here so tentatively is remembered in the completely confident and final statements of 'Little Gidding'. And from the delicacy of this introductory passage issues the first subject, stated in more assured terms:

> What might have been and what has been
> Point to one end which is always present.

This subject is not expanded to any length, and the assurance of the poet's tone dwindles as he proceeds. A brief, perplexed bridge passage follows, and then comes the second subject, taking us into 'our first world'—and we are not dealing, as Eliot has reminded us, 'with the lifetime of one man only', but with our common heritage. This second subject is as tentatively put forward as the first, though it is not tentative for the same reason: we are not here concerned, as before we were, with doubtful metaphysical propositions, but with images, which, though they are perceived as from a great distance, are yet for a time within the poet's grasp, and capable of expansion. Accordingly, the subject is developed at some length, until it abruptly dies, and the movement ends with a simple repetitive coda.

The second, slow movement, opens with a lyric which, although in its actual form it seems very different, fulfils the same function as the descriptive passage beginning 'The chair she sat in, like a burnished throne', in 'The Waste Land'. This passage was an attempt to convey by accumulative description what we are later told by means of a dramatic dialogue, that the Belladonna's life is quite fruitless and futile: and in the same way Eliot is here trying to explain indirectly, by means of 'sense-impression', as Raymond Preston has it, what he afterwards proceeds to tell us by direct statement: 'At the still point of the turning world, neither flesh nor fleshless'. It is apparent that this lyric and this statement constitute the two subjects of the movement, which concludes with a repetition of something that has been said before, but is now made to point to a very different conclusion, that

> involved with past and future
> Only through time time is conquered.

With the second movement the third is to be contrasted, for it deals with 'a place of disaffection', while we have been reading of 'the moment in the arbour where the rain beat', a place of quite an opposite significance. This movement is rather an incantation than a dance, and has two clearly defined subjects, the first, that of the 'strained, time-ridden faces', developed at some length, the second, concerned with 'the world of perpetual solitude', necessarily terse and concentrated. They are presented quite simply, and the poet returns upon the first subject only in order to bring the movement to its close.

We have now explored quite fully the two statements which had been propounded in the first movement: the 'one end, which is always present' has been examined and brought more nearly within our apprehension as 'the still point of the turning world', and the theme 'human kind cannot bear very much reality' has been expanded, inasmuch as we have stood face to face with the world moving 'in appetency, on its metalled ways.' Having completed his expansion of the themes of the first movement, Eliot gives us, as in 'The Waste Land', a fourth movement which serves concisely to sum up what his investigations have revealed, and which thus leaves him free to proceed to his conclusions. This section 'is an imagined participation in the condition of detachment . . . with a glimpse, in a flash of light of its goal'[1] and is expressed in a single symbol. It remains still to be stated, however, how this goal may be reached, and this is the purpose of the fifth section: Eliot's conclusions are two, first that

> Only by the form, the pattern
> Can words or music reach
> The stillness

and second, that, as far as 'human kind' are concerned

> The detail of the pattern is movement,

and being expanded as to their implications, these form the subjects of his closing movement. In dealing here with his own poetry, Eliot is returning to a theme which he has used before, at the beginning of this poem, with 'My words echo, Thus in your mind', and when he says that 'even while the dust moves, there rises the hidden laughter of children in the foliage', he is reminding us of the second subject of his first movement, where he was engaged 'Disturbing the dust on a bowl of rose leaves'. Thus the poem closes with a recapitulation of the central themes which have been used in its composition, though a crescendo and roll of drums like that which concluded 'The Waste Land' would here have been inappropriate.

'Burnt Norton' starts from the hypothetical assumption that what a man needs is detachment, proceeds to examine first the vision which detachment brings with it, then to expose the futility of their activities, who refuse thus to discipline themselves, and brings us so far on our way as to tell us that movement is the shaping force in the pattern of a man's life. Eliot does not expand this last statement, preferring to cement it by references to the mystery of desire and love, and to his initial symbol of the children: thus his conclusion, though it serves as evidence to support the metaphysical postulates with which the poem begins, is not really final, and it is the function of 'East Coker' to examine it in more detail. The 'silent motto' with which 'East Coker' opens establishes its relation to the closing lines of 'Burnt Norton', for 'In my beginning is my end' implies an unswervable but perpetually moving pattern. The poem progresses from a general survey of the rhythm of life to an examination and a refutation of the wisdom of age, from which a further conclusion as to the central theme is drawn, that 'the pattern is new in every moment'. After the recapitulatory fourth movement, Eliot offers us the discoveries he has made in the course of his second examination, that 'there is only the fight to recover what has been lost' in life, and that there is 'a lifetime burning in every moment' of a man's existence. And the poem closes with Eliot's conclusion that 'we must be still and still moving', with a reference to 'the dark cold and empty desolation' of history, thus introducing what is to be the

---

[1] Raymond Preston, *Four Quartets Rehearsed*.

subject of 'The Dry Salvages'. For it is a purpose of this poem to make clear the connexion between the river of life and the ocean of history, in order that we may be aware that

> the past has another pattern, and ceases to be a mere sequence or even development,

and, on the other hand, that

> On whatever sphere of being
> The mind of a man may be intent
> At the time of death—that is the one action
> (And the time of death is every moment).

From his survey of the Annunciation of history, Eliot is able to come to the main conclusion of 'The Dry Salvages', and of the 'Quartets' as a whole, that the central, barely attainable, activity of a man's life should be to endeavour

> . . . to apprehend
> The point of intersection of the timeless
> With time,

which is too difficult a task for most of us, who are content if our own lives are fruitful within the pattern of existence which has been put before us in the first section of 'East Coker'. We have now made the discovery which it was our central purpose in setting out on our voyage to make, and with 'Little Gidding' are returned to more navigable waters. The theme of this poem is the 'temporal reversion' of the last lines of 'The Dry Salvages', and the poet returns upon those earlier themes of the lacerations of old age, and the apparent meaninglessness of history: we may be unable to investigate these mysteries, but if we 'kneel where prayer has been valid' before the evidence of 'the inter-section of the timeless moment': if we are

> restored by that refining fire
> Where you must move in measure, like a dancer,

we shall be able to rejoice.[2]

It was necessary to unify these several elements into a single whole, which could not possibly be a direct and epic sequence of statements. The subject for one thing did not suit with such a method of treatment, the poems constituting a kind of voyage of exploration into the abstract: and so many asides and excursions were needed for Eliot to make his meaning clear, that a conventional narrative order of presentation would have seemed the merest excuse for a poetry of digressions. Eliot has therefore cast his poems in sonata form and as I have demonstrated with

---

[2] A longer and much more satisfactory prose argument of the 'Quartets' is that by B. Rajan in the *Focus Three*.

'Burnt Norton', the relation of each part to its whole is that of music.
Thus the first movement of 'East Coker' contains two subjects, connected by a long bridge passage which serves to set a scene, the first
sketching the 'rise and fall' of human activity, the second a definite
scene, that of 'the open field. . . . On a summer midnight': thus also 'The
Dry Salvages', giving us first a general survey of the course and
attributes of 'the river', then a clear and powerful scene on the sea-
coast: and 'Little Gidding' likewise, with the symbolic picture of the
village in the throes of 'midwinter spring', and the explanation of the
purpose which would direct the visitor to that place. In every case the
first subject is put forward comparatively shortly, the second developed
at some length, and the central point of the movement is revealed
during the course of this development. The second movement in each
of the four poems consists of a lyric and a statement (though the statement takes the form of a dramatic scene in 'Little Gidding') which lyric
and statement stand for the two subjects, the movement reaching its
climax in the development of the statement. The tension which has
mounted during the first two movements is in every case eased in the
more digressive third, whose argument is presented in a looser form,
with the aid of what Mr C. Day Lewis would call fluid imagery. Thus in
'East Coker' we meet with the three symbols of the 'theatre', the
'underground train' and the operating theatre, all of which stand for the
same thing, death: in 'Little Gidding' the movement is even divided,
quite sharply, into two parts, each with its distinctive rhythm and
imagery. The fourth movement is always a recapitulation, a summing-
up of the first three, in their implications, within a single symbol, and
the last, as in music, is made to present the poet's conclusions, to reintroduce the central themes of what has preceded it, and to give us
some intimation of what is to follow. In 'Little Gidding', the last movement is completely final, and themes from each of the 'Quartets' reappear, in order that Eliot may build up a truly comprehensive
conclusion.

It is apparent from this brief survey that the 'Quartets' are not only
dependent upon a single principle, that of sonata form, but also inter-
dependent. I have noted how Eliot prepares the way for each important
new symbol, as when the sea of 'The Dry Salvages' appears in the preceding poem 'East Coker', invested in its full symbolic significance, not
only as the 'vast waters of the petrel and the porpoise' of that poem's
last movement, but also in its first section in the lines

>   Out at sea the dawn wind
>   Wrinkles and slides. I am here
>   Or there, or elsewhere. In my beginning.

Eliot has also taken pains to connect his quartets one with another by
means of recurrent themes and symbols. Thus the second subject in
the second movement of each of the last three quartets is concerned with

old age: in 'East Coker' we have Eliot's analysis of the 'folly' of old men, in 'The Dry Salvages' he discourses on how

> it seems, as one becomes older
> that the past has another pattern . . .

and in 'Little Gidding' are disclosed 'the gifts reserved for age'. Again, the symbol of the railway train appears in the third movement of 'Burnt Norton', with its London tube scene, in the third movement of 'East Coker', where the train 'stops too long between stations', and in 'The Dry Salvages' at the same point we hear of how 'the train starts, and the passengers are settled'. I do not think that this is accidental, and it is worth pointing out that with the broader field of vision of 'The Dry Salvages' comes a slight adjustment of the symbol: the poet is here no longer writing of the underground, but of the long-distance railway. A more important recurrence of theme comes in the last paragraph of each poem. 'Burnt Norton' tells us that 'the detail of the pattern is movement', from 'East Coker' Eliot concludes that 'we must be still and still moving', the theme is fully investigated at the climax of 'The Dry Salvages':

> Here the past and future
> Are conquered, and reconciled,
> Where action were otherwise movement
> Of that which is only moved
> And has in it no source of movement.

and consequently there is in 'Little Gidding' mention of:

> The stillness
> Between two waves of the sea.

This repetition, both of symbol and of theme, serves a double purpose. First, it serves to cement the unity of the 'Quartets', to enable us to make those connections necessary for the consideration of the work as a whole, a definite progression towards one single end. In this way, it fulfils roughly the same function as the nature-myths in 'The Waste Land', though it is a much more subtle and less protrusive device. Second, it provides us with definite landmarks upon which we can be sure that each separate poem will touch. For the 'Quartets' are not one poem as we have come to conceive of a poem, they are rather four concentric circles, each with a slightly larger radius than its predecessor, and each cutting the same straight lines at a slightly different point. Eliot expands his vision from poem to poem, exploring the pattern of the individual in 'Burnt Norton', the pattern of mankind in 'East Coker', the pattern of history in 'The Dry Salvages', and returning upon his tracks in 'Little Gidding' with a vision which serves to transfigure even the London scene of that poem, which is made to bear troubled witness of God in its very unearthliness 'at the recurrent end of the unending'. It cannot be too strongly stressed that the central motive of these poems is their time argument, upon which symbol, lyric, and direct statement are gradually brought to bear: and it is for this reason that the last movement of each poem, as I have shown, returns to the theme of stillness and motion. Eliot explores each of his themes—the individual, the species, and history—in several different ways, by symbolic representation, by examining the evidence which old age affords in relation to the particular theme he is unravelling, and by more or less personal testimony. And he uses the same methods in the same order in each case, as a kind of guarantee that the conclusions he draws will not be arbitrary. . . .

From *Six Essays on the Development of T. S. Eliot*, Fortune Press, 1948, pp. 54–60.

JOHN F. DANBY

Language and Manner in the *Four Quartets*

... Mr Eliot has always been a poet in transit. Yet his transitions have always been returns upon himself. It is possible to see all his poetry as a single poem. The 'Four Quartets' are as necessary to an understanding of 'The Waste Land' as 'The Waste Land' is necessary to prepare for the 'Quartets'. In the 'Quartets' Eliot deliberately takes the greatest of all poetic risks. He includes himself among the poets he is prepared to quote and even parody. The 'Quartets' in this as in much beside indicate a new access of that old nerve which made 'Prufrock' and *Sweeney Agonistes* so shocking and so exciting. They incorporate, too, 'Ash Wednesday' and the 'Ariel' poems and the undigested portions of the poetic dramas. In manner they recapitulate and extend the styles of the early and middle periods.

This paradox of sameness and novelty, consistency and unexpectedness, advance and return, is of course the normal paradox of growth. The figure of the poet in the poetry of the thirty years remains still, as good sculpture remains still. Like good sculpture, too, it rotates, making the reader turn with it and turn round it, leaving him unsatisfied with anything less than the full three-dimensional experience. It is the familiar phenomenon of very great poetry. It is, for example, what Ben Jonson observed in Shakespeare:

> That he
> Who casts to write a living line, must sweat,
> (Such as thine are) and strike the second heat
> Upon the Muses anvile: turne the same,
> (And himselfe with it) that he thinkes to frame.

The 'Four Quartets' show Mr Eliot to be more than ever a poet in transit. Within their lines the poet is turning himself, and again, as before, with himself turning a whole generation of readers. The 'Quartets' thus make a new assessment necessary—a new assessment of Mr Eliot's 'experiment' and of the English 'tradition' in which it stands. The 'Quartets' require this and also facilitate it. They are themselves both poems and criticisms of poetry. One of their main preoccupations is with the deliberate re-appraisal of what the poet can and should do, with what the human ends and purposes are for poetry in our time.

In the last of the 'Quartets' we are given a short account of Mr Eliot's poetic style:

> where every word is at home,
> Taking its place to support the others,
> The word neither diffident nor ostentatious,
> An easy commerce of the old and new,
> The common word exact without vulgarity
> The formal word precise but not pedantic,
> The complete consort dancing together.

—the reliance on the interdependence of words, the resort to the storehouses of meaning opened by erudition, the time-sense and the sense of experimentalism, the dipping through widely different strata of contemporary as well as historical idiom, the avoidance of timidity and self-display, the acceptance of discipline: the lines condense what many readers have said, and what Mr Eliot has recommended to practitioners in more than one place. They also practice what they preach. 'At home' is a rich and easy commerce with the familiar. 'The *common* word *exact*'—that is an unostentatious and witty conjunction: low words enable one sometimes to avoid periphrasis; then again, the well-worn counter ('common' in the other sense) can be re-stamped and re-issued as good as fresh mintage: 'exact' thus unexpectedly consorting with 'common' both gives and gains support.

But maybe the most typical external feature of Mr Eliot's style is the use of repetition:

> Distracted from distraction by distraction,

or:

> keeping time,
> Keeping the rhythm in their dancing
> As in their living in the living seasons
> The time of the seasons and the constellations
> The time of milking and the time of harvest
> The time of the coupling of man and woman
> And that of beast.

or the repetition of rose and rose-garden, rose-bowl and rose-leaves, throughout a poem or series of poems; or the repetition of a whole passage with a new increment of meaning, as the rose-garden of 'Burnt Norton' is repeated at the end of 'Little Gidding'; or the innumerable repetitions of his own former words and phrases and ideas, a kind of organic memory the poems carry forward with them, a living contact with the past, and a trick that constantly imposes a special discipline on the reader—the discipline not of note-taking and concordance-making, but rather of deciding on the relevance of the echo, and of resisting the temptation to be distracted by cataloguing or distracted by reducing the repetitions to a lowest common factor.

The device takes many forms and serves many purposes. Emphasis, of course, is the first and most obvious. Then there is the liturgical rhythm which it helps to build up. More characteristically, repetition in a new context serves to quicken sometimes a latent meaning the word will bear. Thus 'open field' in 'East Coker' means at first just what it says, the open field as opposed to the built-up area. The second time it is used it suggests also the open field of the Middle Ages or before. The word that can break both ways is a favourite with Mr Eliot. Because of him we have become almost hypersensitive to what Dante called the 'polysemous'. Mr Eliot's technique in this is the same as the googly bowler's. And the good reader is kept wary and alert: the queer 'un is always likely to be sent down:

Words move, music moves
Only in time; but that which is only living
Can only die. Words after speech, reach
Into the silence. Only by the form, the pattern,
Can words or music reach
The stillness, as a Chinese jar still
Moves perpetually in its stillness
Not the stillness of the violin, while the note lasts
Not that only, but the co-existence.

The words here are 'moves' and 'stillness', as polysemous as the word 'present' in the opening paragraph of 'Burnt Norton': stillness as immobility in space and immobility to time; stillness as the immobile whole that is made up of moving parts; stillness as that which contains movement and time and yet is neither and yet cannot be thought of as dead fixity; stillness as completeness, spiritual calm; stillness, finally 'of the violin'. This last quick shift is a sudden and rather disturbing transposition. The normal equivalence would be 'Chinese jar' and 'words or music'—as it is at first. The sudden moving of one frame in the comparison (brought about by equating not the musical notes but the immobile musical instrument with the jar) serves I think to push the whole set of meanings a stage further. The violin cannot be merely the instrument, or it would not be raised to the same level as the jar. The violin is not the music which in some sense it causes. The 'violin' is in fact, I think, suddenly made to stand for the poet himself as maker of the 'words or music'—immobile as cause, container and contemplator of the art, the unmoved mover moving through the processes of production. I am not sure this is at all a helpful, much less a right, solution to the puzzle set by 'violin'. It is characteristic, however, of Mr Eliot's verse to set such puzzles. A steady frame of meaning is no sooner established than it is broken in upon by something demanding a yet larger frame, even if a less steady.

All this is commonplace, and Mr Eliot was doing something like it right at the beginning of his career as a major poet. There is a difference, however, in his developed use of the polysemous word. The clue is given in the term 'co-existence' as applied to meanings. A rich word is not necessarily a word that has more than one sense all of which work at the same time (there are some peculiarly rich words the richness of which is felt to consist in the compact singleness of their meaning). It is not, either, as if the bowler must bowl all six balls at once. The so-called ambiguities of the rich word cannot be put on an arithmetical basis. A clutter of several meanings all happening at once would be merely paralysing. A poem constructed of such words could never begin to move. Rather, the meanings co-exist, and then the words are set in transit over the territory they have admittance to, repetition after repetition being step after step of directed advance into meaning.

Just as Mr Eliot himself is a poet constantly turning—

At the first turning of the second stair
I turned. . . .

—so too with his words. And like him, the words move. They are vehicles for meaning in transit. By the time we have given ourselves to the words (as it might be to the parts of the Chinese jar) their meaning is no longer 'in' the words. Even the words already quoted—themselves both describing and demonstrating how words work—let their meaning move through them and move on. The word 'violin' itself makes a gap in the fence. The appropriate philosophical implication would seem to be that what a word means is always transcendent to the word itself, and transcendent to the whole verbal system. In poems we have to deal with perceptions, not with verbal sensations:

Words strain,
Crack and sometimes break, under the burden,
Under the tension, slip, slide, perish,
Decay with imprecision, will not stay in place,
Will not stay still.

In this respect Mr Eliot's poetry has become more and more abstract, in spite of the fact that the concrete image is as impressively a feature of the 'Quartets' as it was of the early poems (and much more in evidence in his latest period than it was in the period of the 'Ariel' poems). Mr Eliot, of course, at the beginning was already emerging from a context which included Imagism and Symbolism. His early formulations concerning poetry were affected by the modes of thought inevitable to reaction with or against the various aesthetic splinter-parties. He passed into currency the notion of 'dissociated sensibility' (and its converse), the notion of the variegated style, the notion of the 'objective equivalents' of thought and feeling which the poetic craftsman should produce. Such critical ideas were the by-products of his own poetic activity. They were never formulae for the production of poems. Some of us, however, not poets like Mr Eliot, were apt to misunderstand him here. And still there is maybe over-much talk about 'texture' in poetry, over-much hounding of a metaphor, totting up of ambiguities, counting of times the recurrent theme occurs; missing the meaning in our anxiety for the 'poetry', unable to see that 'The poetry does not matter'.

What, it might be relevant to ask, does Mr Eliot mean in this phrase by 'poetry'? One way of seeing what is meant would be to contrast the poetry of the 'Quartets' with that of H. D. or Dr Sitwell, or to place it alongside the poetry of the Metaphysicals which Mr Eliot did so much to reintroduce to the wider poetry public.

The metaphysical conceit is very often in danger of draining attention away from what is being said to the manner of the saying. The very success of the image as an image can impede the transit of meaning it is intended to promote. Here, for example, is a famous passage of Donne:

Our two souls therefore, which are one,
    Though I must goe, endure not yet
A breach, but an expansion,
    Like gold to ayery thinnesse beate.

If they be two, they are two so
    As stiffe twin compasses are two,
Thy soul the fixt foot, makes no show
    To move, but doth, if th' other doe.

And though it in the centre sit,
    Yet when the other far doth rome,
It leanes, and hearkens after it,
    And grows erect, as that comes home.

So wilt thou be to mee, who must
    Like th'other foot, obliquely runne;
Thy firmnes drawes my circle just,
    And makes me end where I begunne.

This is finely successful and not uncharacteristic of Donne. At the same time it is apparent, I think, that here Donne's manner is at odds with his matter. The last two lines would be excellent in isolation. Taken with what has preceded them they constitute a worrying snarl in the sense. Unlike Mr Eliot's 'violin', the hitch results in a diminution rather than an extension of the meanings operating through the passage. 'And makes me end where I begunne' is powerful and meaningful. We know what Donne is driving at in the lines generally. Placed as the phrase is, however, it tends to work against the poet's meaning rather than for it. The image of the completed circumference of the circle imposed on us by the preceding verses does not resolve the dichotomies of 'there and here', of presence and absence, of distance and nearness, as it is intended it should. Number is not there slain in love as it is in 'The Phoenix and the Turtle', or as number in a similar connection is obliterated in the 'Four Quartets'. The 'metaphysical' meanings of the last line will not develop in such proximity to the image of the compasses as they find themselves. To discover how best their full development can be promoted we need the 'Quartets' to instruct us—all those careful adjustments and re-adjustments which 'East Coker' makes before

In my beginning is my end

can become:

In my end is my beginning.

The metaphysical conceit is sometimes too definite. It is sometimes a jig-saw that will only fit together in one way, and the multiplicity of its parts does not disguise the restrictedness of its meaning. There is often local and elaborate richness with a corresponding loss of general availability and adaptability. Similarly, the imagism of H. D. can be self-defeating. As Coleridge reminds us, there is a 'dictatorship of the eye' which serves to regiment everything else out of existence. Mr Eliot is well aware of this. He is, of course, a master of the concrete image—the hands dicing in the doorway, the smells of steak in passage-ways, the ragged claws on the sea-bed, the fog that rubs its back against the window-pane. He can use such imagery to suggest a scene or, in series, to define the complexities of a mood—finding objective correlatives to feelings or thoughts. But his developed style goes further. It uses the image differently. It gives the image an extension of meaning. Rather, it operates with the very tension native to language itself: the tension between words and the meaning of words. It is the kind of thing, I think, which Coleridge had in mind when commenting on a passage of Milton:

> I can understand and allow for an effort of the mind, when it would describe what it cannot satisfy itself with the description of, to reconcile opposites and qualify contradictions, leaving a middle state of the mind more strictly appropriate to the imagination than any other, when it is, as it were, hovering between images. . . . The grandest efforts of poetry are where the imagination is called forth, not to produce a distinct form but a strong working of the mind.

As opposed to the poetry of imagery-for-its-own-sake, in which meaning is clotted in garlic and sapphire of the mud, Mr Eliot's poetry is abstract. It is non-sensuous. It does not stay still. Even the separate meanings we can descry and steady our minds on are meant to convey the movement of a larger meaning which flows through them. Words move,

And the detail of the pattern is movement.

The latest poetry of the 'Quartets' is poetry of a Coleridgean 'middle state of the mind', as the Donne passage is not, and as even the poetry of 'The Waste Land' does not succeed in becoming. The rose-garden at the end of 'Little Gidding' is the same as that presented at the beginning of 'Burnt Norton', but it works to a different meaning, it points in an opposite direction. Mr Eliot himself underlines for us the new element in his attitude to language:

> So here I am, in the middle way, having had twenty years,
> Twenty years largely wasted, the years of *l'entre deux guerres*,
> Trying to learn to use words, and every attempt
> Is a wholly new start, and a different kind of failure
> Because one has only learnt to get the better of words
> For the thing one no longer has to say or the way in which
> One is no longer disposed to say it.

. . . The abstract quality of Mr Eliot's latest poetry, then, consists in a transcendence of the sensuous in words, and in a use of the imagery of the will—the kinetic imagery of movement and tension. It tries to lend itself to the process rather than to utilize the products. It assumes at the outset that words are limited: they move, slip, slide and perish—and they do this because they are floating on the stream of meaning. To seize the word is to lift it out of the current whose course it indicates. The only thing to do is to utilize the apparent limitations of words. Mr Eliot's poetry, therefore, takes this movement for granted and then uses it as the very basis of the technique of expression. It knows that words support each other and require each other for the maintaining and defining of their movement. It knows too that to repeat a word is the safest way of drawing attention to the very transit of meaning inside a word. The repetitions exhaust the circuits words in their movement can describe. The detail of the pattern is movement. And yet the whole pattern itself does not stay still. It is itself a further reaching, a kind of prayer. Movement is mounted upon movement. . . .

From *The Cambridge Journal*, Vol. 4, No. 2, 1950, pp. 707–15.

JOHN PETER

Murder in the Cathedral

Like a Greek tragedy (it is of course the classical rather than the Elizabethan tradition we are conscious of here) *Murder in the Cathedral* opens with a Chorus, that of the Women of Canterbury, and like its Attic counterpart this Chorus gives us a good deal of information (often simply atmospheric) about the time, place and potentiality of the scene. The immediate emphasis is obvious:

> Are we drawn by danger? Is it knowledge of safety, that draws our feet
> Towards the cathedral?

Eliot uses a seeming contradiction, characteristically, to stress the point. We are aware at once that there is both danger and safety and that, though hyperconscious of it, the Chorus know that the danger only indirectly threatens them:

> There is no danger
> For us.

Twice that 'For us' is emphasized at the beginning of a line. The Chorus are, as they realize, initially present merely as lookers-on, and they put an accent on their own impotence by speaking of their limbs and organs as if these were out of their direct control:

> Some presage of an act
> Which our eyes are compelled to witness, has forced our feet
> Towards the cathedral.

Quickly the atmosphere of strain and expectancy is evoked, a simple visual image being loaded from line to line with more and more significance:

> While the labourer kicks off a muddy boot and stretches his hand to the fire,
> The New Year waits, destiny waits for the coming.
> Who has stretched out his hand to the fire and remembered the Saints at All Hallows,
> Remembered the martyrs and saints who wait? and who shall
> Stretch out his hand to the fire, and deny his master?

The interest shifts from Peter (and Christ) to Thomas. We are told that he 'was always kind to his people' but that 'it would not be well if he should return'. It becomes clear that it is he whom the danger threatens, and with this knowledge the position of the Chorus also clarifies.

This is ambivalent. At one level they are simply the poor women of Canterbury, immersed in the routine of existence and fearful lest anything should occur to upset that routine. Like the labourer, with his orthopterous colour adaptation—he who

> bends to his piece of earth, earth-colour, his own colour,
> Preferring to pass unobserved—

their dominant effort is to efface themselves, to avoid being implicated in any of the dangerous actions that are afoot. To appreciate this fully is crucial, for it is in terms of the modification of this attitude that much of the significance of the 'murder' is embodied and expressed. Salvation is presented, not by talking about it . . . but by showing it operating in the consciousness of the Chorus. Again, at another level the Chorus are transparently more than their natural selves. Like their equivalents in Greek tragedy they present a commentary on the action, anticipating and preparing us for developments, rousing us, with their passionate dithyrambs, to participate wholeheartedly in the emotional crises that arise, supplying the action with a background that is, like music, all-pervasive. It is in this their second role, that they now speak of movements of vision 'in a shaft of sunlight', and it is as a flash of clairvoyance that their concluding apostrophe to December is made:

> Shall the Son of Man be born again in the litter of scorn?

For all its specificity this is wide enough to suggest Thomas' own case and the redemption which is in turn to be made possible through his martyrdom. Meantime the Chorus fall silent—and the priests enter upon the stage.

> For us, the poor, there is no action,
> But only to wait and to witness—

Almost at once the tone of the verse alters. This is emphasized by the First Priest's use of two of the Chorus' lines. Significantly the next line ('He who was always kind to his people') is not given and the Priests fall to discussing the temporal effects of Thomas' return with the Messenger, speaking of his pride and isolation, gladly affirming that he will tell them what to do. Although there is nothing in the treatment of these characters that can be called positively unsympathetic I think this section is designed (apart from its content of sheer information) to show that it is not primarily for such at these that Thomas will die. The Priests are presented almost as sanguine and certainly as being capable of taking care of themselves. Their piety is tinged with worldliness and they have just enough cynicism to quote loosely from Ecclesiastes, abandoning themselves to a flux of external events:

> For good or ill, let the wheel turn.
> The wheel has been still, these seven years, and no good.

G

For ill or good, let the wheel turn.
For who knows the end of good or evil?
Until the grinders cease
And the door shall be shut in the street,
And all the daughters of music shall be brought low.

This fidgety acceptance of mere change is what the Chorus criticize as they burst out again. They know that the present is perilous and a change for the better hardly possible:

Ill the wind, ill the time, uncertain the profit, certain the danger.

They appeal to Thomas to return to France:

You come with applause, you come with rejoicing, but you come bringing death into Canterbury:
A doom on the house, a doom on yourself, a doom on the world.

To them, who 'do not wish anything to happen', who go on 'living and partly living', Thomas' return seems only to presage catastrophe. From the first touch of sharpness ('our brains unskinned like the layers of an onion') the intensity of their foreboding increases. When they have done the Second Priest reproves them for croaking (isn't the image rather a comment on him than on them?) 'like frogs in the treetops'. Thomas, entering, reproves him in turn.

Peace. And let them be, in their exaltation.
They speak better than they know, and beyond your understanding.
They know and do not know, what it is to act or suffer.
They know and do not know, that action is suffering
And suffering is action. Neither does the agent suffer
Nor the patient act. But both are fixed
In an eternal action, an eternal patience
To which all must consent that it may be willed
And which all must suffer that they may will it,
That the pattern may subsist, for the pattern is the action
And the suffering, that the wheel may turn and still
Be forever still.

This is likely to be dismissed as Eliotese, and perhaps with some reason; but its extreme inexplicitness is not arbitrary, the passage being kept deliberately ambiguous so as to allow it to be spoken again a little later on, in a completely different context, without seeming irrelevant there. Some 'small matters' are discussed, and Thomas speaks of his crossing and its political significance. And at this stage the drama enters upon a new development.

The material facts of the situation being now adequately suggested, Eliot's next endeavour is equally to present the repercussions that they occasion in Thomas' mind. The remainder of Part One anatomizes these. It does so, not by the Elizabethan technique of soliloquy, but through a technique of allegory or 'objectification' that is close to that of the *autos* of Calderón[1] It is typical of Eliot's early meticulousness (it has worn thin since, I fear) that he should mark the transition from one reality to another unambiguously: here he does it by modulating into those terse, Anglo-Saxon-like locutions which are so often in other modern poets merely idiosyncratic. Hearing the articles begin to disappear from Thomas' speech ('End will be simple, sudden, God-given') and the abruptness with which he concludes ('All things prepare the event. Watch.') we are prepared for the First Tempter, who enters at once. He is the first of three whom, since their temptations offer only temporal and material benefits, Thomas finds it fairly easy to resist. They are introduced, these three, partly to show the truth of Thomas' saying,

> The impossible is still temptation,

partly to give added point to what succeeds. . . .

The fourth Tempter, entering with congratulations, is at once endowed with a more sinister import. 'Who are you?' Thomas asks. 'I expected Three visitors, not four.' Meeting with no answer more definite than 'I always precede expectation' he is forced to ask the question again, and again it is evaded. The two figures hold the stage, fencing cautiously with their speeches. Thomas is suspicious, we can see, and especially since the Tempter seems to be stating a case with which he can only agree. Counselled to

> Think of pilgrims, standing in line
> Before the glittering jewelled shrine

he replies (the line is something of an actor's crux):

> I have thought of these things.

The Tempter confuses him with obliquities; then his advice becomes more explicit:

> Seek the way of martyrdom, make yourself the lowest
> On earth, to be high in heaven.
> And see far off below you, where the gulf is fixed,

---

[1] Compare A. A. Parker, *The Allegorical Drama of Calderón* (1942), pp. 82–3: 'They [the *autos*] deal with another plane of experience; they are conceptual and not realistic. . . . This is what Calderón in his later *autos* so often does: he allows his audience to follow each step in the train of thought as it emerges from the mind of a character on the stage actually conceiving the action before their eyes. The importance of this strikingly original device lies in the remarkable clarity it can give to an abstract theme. . . .' I suppose we may recall what Harry says in *The Family Reunion*:

> Perhaps my life has only been a dream
> Dreamt through me by the minds of others.

Your persecutors, in timeless torment,
Parched passion, beyond expiation.

With this Thomas begins to see what the temptation involves—an
ultimate vitiation of his martyrdom through hypocrisy—and he bursts
out:

No!
Who are you, tempting with my own desires?
. . . Others offered real goods, worthless
But real. You only offer
Dreams to damnation.

With the Tempter's retort ('You have often dreamt them') and
Thomas' appeals to be freed from the damning weight of his pride, we
reach the point—and it should in its way be almost blood-curdling—
where the Tempter quotes to Thomas his own words, noticed earlier,
concerning action and suffering. This is a device, classic in its neatness,
to show how inextricably mixed Thomas' motives still remain. We see
that the whole dialogue with the Tempters has symbolized an intro-
spective process and that hitherto it has been a comparatively simple
matter for the Archbishop to isolate and discard the temptations. Now,
however, tempter and tempted begin to merge: Thomas is no longer the
vigilant custodian over his own mind but is involved in a tangle of
motives which he himself can only partially analyse. Some external
prompting is needed to help him to his final decision.

This comes, as it must, from the Chorus, his spiritual dependents.
After an orchestral *crescendo* of doubt and confusion Thomas is shown
listening to their clamourous hopelessness, image after image in their
speech suggesting a single sense of horror and panic—

The forms take shape in the dark air:
Puss-purr of leopard, footfall of padding bear,
Palm-pat of nodding ape, square hyaena waiting,
For laughter, laughter, laughter. The Lords of Hell are here.

It is with their last cry, identifying their own balance between hope and
despair with his decision, that resolution breaks across his hesitancy.

O Thomas Archbishop, save us, save us, save yourself that we may
   be saved;
Destroy yourself and we are destroyed.

THOMAS
Now is my way clear, now is the meaning plain. . . .

The archbishop, to sum up the matter tersely, here realizes that his
decision is no longer personal or autonomous. Involved in the integrity
with which he must resolve the struggle in his own conscience is the

spiritual integrity and well-being of the whole Church, and particularly of these members of it, the women of Canterbury. But a terse comment like this does scant justice to the dramatic effectiveness at this point. That the poet should have been able to make his point so clearly, while at the same time, through the dextrous orchestration of the voices, preserving all the dramatic suspense latent in the situation, is surely very much to his credit. Such a marriage of poetry and excitement is a far cry from the verbose inertia of the poetic dramas of the nineteenth century.

Thomas, his decision achieved, is allowed to address the audience briefly—a gesture which is useful, technically, to suggest that the act is now nearly over, and also to anticipate the direct address of the Interlude. Then the curtain falls on a scene of resignation in which we see him finally and irrevocably dedicated to what he now recognizes as his necessary purpose:

Now my good Angel, whom God appoints
To be my guardian, hover over the swords' points.

It is a good curtain and indeed, to my mind, a good act. Few verse dramatists of the past three hundred years have been able to see so clearly what is to be done; fewer still have been able, having perceived it, so precisely and effectively to get it done. There is a touch here that English drama has not felt since the Jacobeans—something which, when one remembers the precedents Eliot had in 1935, is all the more remarkable.

Perhaps what follows can be treated rather more summarily. It will be appreciated that by the end of Part I the play is (at least in one, not unimportant respect) virtually over. The fundamental implications of the action are now clearly before us and it only remains for the dramatist to show the factual outcome of the inward struggle, Thomas' visible death and its effects. I do not think Eliot had any illusions about the danger of a drop in emotional temperature at this point, for it seems to be deliberately that he introduces several technical developments in the central and later sections of the play. One feels that these are diversionary, designed to hold an interest which might otherwise begin to flag. It is only at the end, when a richer and less explicit significance returns to the action, that the *ars* is once more *celare artem.* . . .

When the Knights have finished speaking we feel sincerity in a deeper dimension return with a perceptible jar. I feel the treatment here, in the conclusion of the play, is again reminiscent of a technique in music. The 'theme' is stated quite fully in the speeches given to the Priests and there is, in what we might call a ratiocinative or factual sense, little to add to these. They explain how the Church has been strengthened by Thomas' death, how the Knights are now reduced to spiritual suicide, how the Archbishop is already translated. But there is, as yet, no emotional resolution. As in a musical recapitulation this material is immediately restated, this time with all the emphasis the poet can command. For the first time the Chorus becomes resonantly affirmative, sounding their praises of God in terms of a creation that has lost all its frightfulness. The purring leopard, the patting ape, the waiting hyena—these are all recognized as necessary units in an intelligible whole, implying, even by negation, the glory of God:

The darkness declares the glory of light.

Once again a martyr has redeemed the crumbling faith, and now the Chorus are free to sing triumphantly of what before they had so dreaded, the act of death and the benison proceeding from it. Gradually, in strong, liturgical rhythms, they build a firm statement of this recaptured peace, their voices falling silent upon an epitome which cannot but be impressive to whoever has attended the full meaning of the play:

Blessed Thomas, pray for us.

Only by virtue of his martyrdom is Thomas 'Blessed'; only by virtue of what they had flinched from do the women of Canterbury now have an intermediary and advocate with God. There is true Aristotelian *peripeteia* here; and there is also, it seems to me, an economy and vitality of statement that no modern reader or theatre-goer should be encouraged to neglect. . . .

From *The Sewanee Review*, Vol. 61, 1953, pp. 366–71.

CAROL H. SMITH

The Family Reunion

Between the time of *Sweeney Agonistes* and *The Family Reunion* Eliot learned more about dramatic writing[1] and, while his basic ideals were unchanged, he had modified his ideas about dramatic rhythm and dramatic poetry. He had learned from *The Rock* and *Murder in the Cathedral* what audiences might be expected to respond to and in his first work written specifically for the commercial theatre he attempted to put into effect his conclusion that poetic drama must compete directly with the realistic theatre on that theatre's own terms. It will be remembered that while Eliot had continued to treat the theme of sainthood and the conflict of worldly and spiritual power in *Murder in the Cathedral*, he came to feel that he had been led away from his intention of creating a drama of contemporary relevance using the language of modern life; both the 'neutral' language and the historical situation made the play seem to him a 'dead end'.[2] He was still determinedly against the pretence of stage realism, and the social and psychological themes of the modern stage, just as he was still opposed to both prose and the conventional metres of dramatic verse. His first full-scale attempt to resolve the dilemmas in which he found himself is to be seen in *The Family Reunion*.

In an effort to compete with the commercial theatre and to meet his audience on their own ground while avoiding violations of his views on drama, he decided on a new method of handling dramatic levels—a way which might satisfy both his audience and himself at the same time. In *Murder in the Cathedral* he had been successful in sustaining two distinct levels of meaning, the surface actions leading to the martyrdom of Becket and beneath the surface the analogies with the suffering and glory of Christ. The levels were openly merged and communicated to the Cathedral audience at key points in the dramatic structure, such as in Becket's sermon and in the final chorus. At other points less obvious methods were employed, including poetic suggestions which might disclose symbolic connections to the enlightened imagination, verbal echoes of Scripture, and even visual theatrical representations, notably the wheel of swords with Becket at the centre. Universality of meaning was conveyed by the ritual sequences embedded in the surface actions

[1] E. Martin Browne has described Eliot's close attention to the craft of theatrical writing in 'From *The Rock* to *The Confidential Clerk*', *T. S. Eliot: A Symposium for His Seventieth Birthday*, ed. Neville Braybrooke, pp. 57–69.

[2] Eliot, *On Poetry and Poets*, pp. 84–5.

and underlying strata. However, the playwright's attempts to make the situation meaningful to the contemporary world were to some degree artificial, as in the final speeches by the Knights and Thomas' occasional addresses to the audience. In *The Family Reunion* relevance to the everyday experience of the audience was to come first but not so much in deference to the expectations of the audience, as in an effort to show them the errors of their expectations. The curtain was to open on the most conventional of dramatic worlds, the English drawing room, but every device at the dramatist's disposal was to be used as the play progressed to shake the audience's confidence in the validity of that world of surface reality as a total representation of existence. This, I believe, was the rationale behind the many 'violations' of the theatre of realism which disturbed both audiences and critics of this play.

Thus the normality of the everyday world of the play is continually disrupted. In the surface action, the family (and audience) is gathered in expectation of one kind of reunion, but finds another kind of union portrayed. Characters, such as the aunts and uncles, who begin by speaking the most ordinary prose sentiments, break into choral chants; scenes, such as that between Mary and Harry, which begin in the expectation of romance or 'love interest', end in rejection of human love in favour of the love of God. Most startling of all and contrived to shatter confidence in the most sacred of dramatic conventions, the belief in the reality of the make-believe occurring on stage, is the appearance of the Eumenides, a 'shock-tactic' comparable to the Knights' address to the modern audience in *Murder in the Cathedral*.

Amid the many disruptions, it was necessary to present a coherent guide to the meaning of the action beneath the surface events. This function was served by the use of the Orestes myth and the religious ritual implicit in it. The total effect was intended to be the presentation of a modern counterpart to the universal experience of religious purgation. The audience was to leave the theatre having seen an action in modern existence which duplicated the age-old religious pattern and returned to the theatre its original function of expressing God's presence.[3]

Along with the modifications in setting and poetic language came a somewhat more positive conception of the purgative way in the treatment of the hero's spiritual dilemma. In *Sweeney Agonistes* only the negative side, the horror and desolation of the spiritual pursuit, was emphasized, together with the barrenness of temporal existence; in *The Family Reunion* there is a recognition that the period of desolation is a preparation for a more positive stage of final union with the divine

---

[3] Audience reaction would indicate that Eliot was overly optimistic in his confidence that audiences would give up either belief in dramatic conventions or confidence in the reality of the external, visible world. Grover Smith, speculating on the audience's reaction to the play, comments: 'The audience, if not just giddy by now, leaves the theatre with perhaps a suspicion that it has been intellectually "had" ' (*T. S. Eliot's Poetry and Plays*, p. 208).

principle. To be sure, the drama ends before Harry has reached that state of union, but it is made clear that he has passed through his worst suffering, the period during which he felt terror in the presence of his Furies because he did not understand their mission.

Interrelated with this new emphasis is the new role played by such characters as Agatha and Mary and Downing, the 'watchers and waiters' in the spiritual education of the central character. The prominence of these characters represents, it seems to me, an important alteration in the playwright's attitude toward human love. The instruction of St John of the Cross to the penitent to divest himself of the love of created beings before the divine union can take place—an instruction issued significantly at the darkest step of St John's ten stairs—has been replaced in part by Agatha's instructive and curative love. There is, to be sure, a repudiation of human love as represented by Harry's mother's desire to impose her will on his future, by Mary's offer of love which Harry momentarily hopes might save him, and by Harry's wife's attempt to dominate him by her will. Nevertheless, in the character of Agatha, who leads him to the proper recognition of his past and his future through her love for him and thus to the 'other side of despair', there exists a merging of human and divine Love. This new direction has been followed in Eliot's later plays by a succession of characters who are part human, part divine, and who function to show the penitent his way.

Eliot's treatment of the unaware characters also has been gradually modified. In *Sweeney Agonistes* the chorus is barely differentiated, and it expressed its relation to Sweeney's tale of symbolic purgation by its stylized choral chants of terrified recognition of the awfulness of his encounter with divinity. In *Murder in the Cathedral* the somewhat more positive side of the entry of the spiritual is apparent in the final acceptance by the women of Canterbury of the agony and the glory which Thomas' martyrdom brings into their humble lives. They are not, however, individualized or developed as dramatic personalities. In *The Family Reunion* the chorus is made up of individual members of Harry's family who, though they remain relatively flat characters, are individualized by their differing reactions to the hero's dilemma and by the characteristic verse patterns each is given to speak.[4] Since in this play

---

[4] D. E. Jones gives a valuable analysis of the verse patterns of the choral characters in *The Plays of T. S. Eliot*, p. 86: 'The degree of control that the verse gives over characterization and dramatic tension can be illustrated from the scene in which the uncles and aunts discuss 'the younger generation'. . . . Here, the stiff pompous, insensitive rhythm which characterizes Charles, especially in his more obtuse mood, gives way to an ampler, more relaxed, but still circumscribed movement as Gerald makes his kindly gesture. Mary's pent-up emotion reveals itself in a very jerky movement (the repetitions in 'information . . . generation' and 'I don't deserve. . . . I don't belong' are the more obvious means of achieving a kind of stumbling bitterness). The awkward silence which covers her exit is broken by Violet's sharp decisiveness. Gerald's reaction does not go deeper than bemusement; the rhythm has only a slight hesitancy. With

Eliot was still trying for the stylized effect of Ben Jonson's flat characters (to be unaware of the spiritual world equals spiritual flatness in Eliot's plays), these characters are left undeveloped intentionally in order that they may fulfil their function in the microcosmic dramatic world.

Eliot's manipulation of his characters and theme in this multi-level drama becomes clear when the levels are examined and compared. The clash of the natural and supernatural worlds is present on both levels of the drama. The dramatic conflict implicit in the surface action of the play is between two conceptions of reality or, to express it in the play's own terms, between the two conceptions of the family reunion. The family reunion planned by Amy, Dowager Lady Monchensey, is ostensibly in celebration of her birthday but is actually an effort to establish her eldest son Harry in her place as master of Wishwood and head of the family. Her chief adversary in this plan is Harry himself; he has successfully thwarted his mother's plans in the past by his marriage to a woman who would have no part of the family and by his year of wandering since his wife's 'death by water'. In contrast to Amy's conception of the reunion of the family in order to solidify the family's worldly domain is the spiritual reunion which is the goal of Harry's trial. . . .

When Harry leaves Wishwood it is at the cost of his mother's life. She realizes that she has lost her battle to keep her son, and she is incapable of understanding that the ways of divine love take precedence over the ways of human love. Harry's decision to accept his calling even at the price of his 'murder' of his mother is endorsed by Agatha. Her line:

> Love compels cruelty
> To those who do not understand love[5]

might well stand as the modification of the instruction of St John of the Cross which *The Family Reunion* expresses. Although human love is now not altogether denied, it is accepted only in so far as it provides a means to achieving reunion with God.

At the close of the play, Harry's reunion has won out over his mother's.[6] Agatha's summary of the play's climax is intended to express the symbolic meaning of the events portrayed:

his stolid complacency, Charles moves firmly in to put Mary's outburst into perspective, as he would think. And, finally, Amy with her characteristically domineering rhythm closes the incident. The tenacious rhythm of her monosyllabic half-line 'but life may still go right' prevents us from interpreting it as mere wish; she clearly intends to do what she can to make it go right. The scene demonstrates that poetic drama can have something of the precision of a musical score. Character and dramatic structure are here integrated in the verse rhythm, through which the tension of the awkward moment is built up and resolved.'

[5] Eliot, *Complete Poems and Plays*, p. 279.

[6] There have been a number of complaints registered against the ending of *The Family Reunion*. Grover Smith, in *T. S. Eliot's Poetry and Plays*, p. 200, has objected to the absence of specific information about what will happen to

What we have written is not a story of detection,
Of crime and punishment, but of sin and expiation.
It is possible that you have not known what sin
You shall expiate, or whose, or why. It is certain
That the knowledge of it must precede the expiation.
It is possible that sin may strain and struggle
In its dark instinctive birth, to come to consciousness
And so find expurgation. It is possible
You are the consciousness of your unhappy family,
Its bird sent flying through the purgatorial flame.
Indeed it is possible. You may learn hereafter,
Moving alone through flames of ice, chosen
To resolve the enchantment under which we suffer.[7]

Agatha's comment makes explicit for the audience Harry's divine mission. She also implies that he is to be a kind of sacrificial scapegoat for his entire family. When she addresses him as 'the consciousness of your unhappy family' and suggests that he is 'to resolve the enchantment under which we suffer', she connects his personal identity with all saviours who suffer and are purged of the sins of others. Symbolically, the family on whose behalf he suffers is the family of man.

Agatha's statement that the events of the drama are not a 'story of detection, Of crime and punishment, but of expiation' points out to the audience that the 'thriller'[8] aspect of the play (for example, the sudden visit of the police chief, the family's questioning of Downing, and their other attempts to discover if Harry murdered his wife) is an intentional misrepresentation of events. It is another example of the author's attempt to build up one kind of expectation in the audience only to shatter it with a different and unexpected interpretation of events. In the reference to Dostoevski's *Crime and Punishment* the playwright hints at a precedent for his device, for *Crime and Punishment* also begins as a murder

Harry after the curtain falls. (Michael Redgrave asked Eliot the same question during rehearsal for the London production and is reported to have received the reply that Harry and his chauffeur 'go off and get jobs in the East End'! [D. E. Jones, *The Plays of T. S. Eliot*, p. 101.]) F. O. Matthiessen has raised a more serious objection which reveals the same disposition to overlook the 'allegorical' quality of the events. He objects to Harry's lack of humanity in his treatment of his mother (*The Achievement of T. S. Eliot*, pp. 170–1). The surfaces of Eliot's plays are intended, I think, to provide fables which carry the attention of the audience to the deeper level of interpretation. The plays are 'abstract' and 'stylized' in the sense Eliot developed in his writings about drama during the nineteen-twenties and cannot be viewed by the standards of the realistic theatre without distorting their meaning. It is my conjecture that one of the reasons behind Eliot's change to a comic surface in his next play, *The Cocktail Party*, was the greater tolerance of audiences for 'abstraction' in comedy than in other dramatic forms.

[7] Eliot, *Complete Poems and Plays*, p. 275.
[8] Eliot's interest in 'thrillers', detective fiction, and crime has been discussed by Grover Smith in *T. S. Eliot's Poetry and Plays*, pp. 116–18, and in 'T. S. Eliot and Sherlock Holmes', *Notes and Queries*, 193, 2 October 1948, 431–2.

mystery and ends as a tale of spiritual purgation. The fact that the *Oresteia* also follows the same pattern suggests the connection of this theme with ritual and myth.

Eliot's use of his mythical source in *The Family Reunion* was prophetic of his method in later plays. The ritual struggle between the dominion of earth and the dominion of heaven provided the fundamental conflict of the play, and the events in Aeschylus' version of the myth provided a situation with dramatic possibilities which the playwright explored in modern terms. . . .

From *T. S. Eliot's Dramatic Theory and Practice*, Princeton and Oxford University Press, 1965, pp. 115–32.

After the Cocktails

Failures, among the works of a great writer, have to be taken seriously; especially if he is such a highly deliberate and self-critical one as T. S. Eliot. It is not merely that, whatever their limitations, such works are nevertheless likely to be of considerable intrinsic interest, but that they will almost inevitably throw light on other aspects of his artistic career. *The Cocktail Party* is certainly among the least satisfying of Eliot's published works. . . .

A brief interpretive summary will be necessary as a basis for discussion. It is suggested that something on the following lines emerges from the pattern of the play:

1. Human relations are either permeated by illusion, or disillusioned, lacking in 'ecstasy'. (i) They are illusory: either because they are rooted in idealizations of the other (as Celia idealizes Edward), or sheer incomprehension of the other (as Peter's spurious understanding of Celia); or self-deception (as Edward's relation to Celia, and—previously—to Lavinia; there is also an element of self-deception in Peter's incomprehension of Celia, on whom he projects his own self-idealization). (ii) If not illusory, they are lacking in 'ecstasy', since they must then grow out of active disillusionment—a state at which all the above characters arrive, and which appears also to be the foundation of Sir Henry Harcourt-Reilly's centrally privileged personality.

2. This state of affairs is not contingent on individual experience; it is part of 'the human condition' (Reilly's phrase); which, at the level of human relations, is one of inescapable aloneness.

REILLY
So you want to see no one?

CELIA
No . . . it isn't that I *want* to be alone,
But that everyone's alone—or so it seems to me.
They make noises, and think they are talking to each other;
They make faces, and think they understand each other.
And I'm sure that they don't. Is that a delusion?

REILLY
A delusion is something we must return from.
There are other states of mind which we take to be delusion,
But which we must accept and go on from.

3. 'Going on' from this 'state of mind' accordingly resolves itself into an *acceptance* of this aloneness—into making 'the best of a bad job':

EDWARD

Lavinia, we must make the best of a bad job.
That is what he means.

REILLY

When you find, Mr Chamberlayne,
The best of a bad job is all any of us make of it—
Except of course, the saints—such as those who go
To the sanatorium—you will forget this phrase,
And in forgetting it will alter the condition.

—though 'the condition' for all such is to:

remember
The vision they have had, but they cease to regret it,
Maintain themselves by the common routine,
Learn to avoid excessive expectation . . .
Become tolerant of themselves and others,
Giving and taking, in the usual actions
What there is to give and take. They do not repine . . .

which, of course, is the 'condition'—the world of pantomime and cocktail parties—in which the Chamberlaynes are left at the end of the play; and, in his different way, Peter, maintaining himself by the common routine at Boltwell ('with a team of experts'), doing a good job of work on a second-rate film:

PETER

I suppose I didn't know her,
I didn't understand her. I understand nothing.

REILLY

You understand your *métier*, Mr Quilpe—
Which is the most that any of us can ask for.

Except of course, the saints—such as those who go to the sanatorium!
4. And this, heroic sanctity, is offered as the *only* alternative to making 'the best of a bad job' at the level of personal relations or of maintaining oneself 'by the common routine'—at Boltwell or elsewhere. That is why it is here rooted in

The kind of faith that issues from despair.

'Communion' is possible only with God. Those who take the 'other' way can '*forget* their loneliness' (they cannot escape it);

You will not forget yours.
Each way means loneliness—and communion.

Both ways avoid the final desolation
Of solitude in the phantasmal world
Of imagination, shuffling memories and desires.

The dichotomy is thus explicitly made absolute. The two ways—

Neither way is better.
Both are necessary. It is also necessary
To make a choice between them—

each involving 'loneliness', are sharply opposed to any attempted
'communion' at other levels. Desire for such communion is vain.
Everyone's alone—except for the transcendent; human relations have
no intrinsic reality or value: their only value (like that of heroic
sanctity) is *instrumental*, leading (provided we can accept them as
valueless in themselves!)

towards possession
Of what you have sought for in the wrong place.

And 'the wrong place' covers a wide area, to be sure: the entire field of
values in time, in so far as they are pursued in and for themselves. It is
the futility of such a pursuit which the earlier part of the play seeks to
establish. These attempts—the usual stuff of life—are revealed as
leading to the familiar entanglements of conventional comedy, or to the
brink of tragedy and despair: indeed, but for Reilly and his assistants, to

the final desolation
Of solitude in the phantasmal world
Of imagination, shuffling memories and desires.

For it is in this 'phantasmal world' that they inhere. Real communion
can only be won by a free acceptance of 'loneliness' one 'way' or
another—complete surrender of temporal fruition.

5. The final implication is surely that Time is entirely corrupt: not
merely fallen and imperfect, and finally subject to the Eternal, but
destitute of any intrinsic positive significance. Those who

do not repine
Are contented with the morning that separates
And with the evening that brings together
For casual talk before the fire
Two people who know they do not understand each other,
Breeding children whom they do not understand
And who will never understand them—

lead 'a good life', Reilly assures Celia;

Though you will not know how good
Till you come to the end.

Its goodness, that is, is exclusively a moral one—and 'moral' in the
narrowest of ways;

In a world of lunacy,
Violence, stupidity, greed . . . it is a good life.

'Good', here, surely for what it will bring—when 'you come to the end';
hardly for what it *is*: to seek its goodness partly in what it is would be to
seek 'in the wrong place'. Love, full-blooded, full-spirited love of
another creature, has emerged as either a projection of the self, or a
projection of infinite, religious, aspirations, into finite symbols for ever
removed from all genuine relation. The sort of natural happiness people
look for in human relationships is thus not merely presented as illusory;
but as a narcissist indulgence in a 'phantasmal world' of self-reflection,
or a pseudo-religious inflation of equally 'phantasmal' temporal exis-
tents. And it is not merely specifically misguided pursuits of such
happiness that are in question but the pursuit as such, wherever it is
for an immediate fulfilment. And so when Celia asks:

Can we only love
Something created by our own imagination?
Are we all in fact unloving and unlovable?
Then one *is* alone, and if one is alone
Then lover and beloved are equally unreal
And the dreamer is no more real than his dreams—

Reilly, though he does not directly assent, does not challenge the suggestion. And the two exclusive alternatives he offers to the unperceived
solitude of illusion are the loneliness of a disillusioned domesticity, so
innocent of 'phantasy' that

you will not know how good
Till you come to the end—

and the loneliness of a 'faith that issues from despair', whose

way leads towards possession
Of what you have sought for in the wrong place.

The possibility of expunging 'illusion' and yet retaining 'ecstasy', of
raising *having* to *being*, *I-It* to *I-Thou*, within the limits of the created
universe, is not allowed to intrude. *Here is a place of disaffection.*
     The disturbing conclusion emerges that *The Cocktail Party* is
(unwittingly) a Manichean play. Its vision is not that of a humane—
'Incarnational' and 'sacramental'—Christianity, but approximates to a
radical division of existence into spheres of Nature and Transcendence
sharply separated from each other: where the transcendent is not merely
approached by way of the disclosure of Nature's essential imperfec-
tions, but finally embraced as a—literally—*desperate alternative* to the
latter's graceless essence.
     Whatever the 'intention' (and at any rate we may be sure that this
does not include the crystallization of Manichean attitudes) some such
result seems indubitably present to us in the play. It is as if, caught in

the boiling-bitter flood of life-revulsion that has gathered to such enormity in our time, Eliot, swept along on its crest, were at the same time composedly—and even somewhat primly—delivering an authoritative sermon on Hope. There is all but no attempt to qualify the sense of self-imprisonment, the desolate unreality of disenchanted existence, *here and now*: where one has

                                        no delusions—
Except that the world I live in seems all a delusion;

—where

Nothing again can either hurt or heal

—and all is

Dry, endless, meaningless, inhuman—

like a heap of broken 'phantasmal' Thou's. 'The horror and the boredom' (significant key words in Eliot's criticism) are not merely *accepted*, as products of the disasters and inadequacies of a plane of being which is nevertheless gifted with life and reality, but are apparently accepted *as sovereign and exclusive principles of temporal existence*. So that those at last 'stripped naked to their souls', if not eligible for 'the sanatorium', will at best

Maintain themselves by the common routine,

in a world of committees, film-making, drawing-room relationships and immaculate husbandly compliments about dresses—

Before a party! And that's when one needs them.

Even if 'the vision they have had' is no longer regretted, 'the horror and the boredom' would appear to be endemic. . . .

This drift towards Manicheism—in its essential revulsion from life, 'yoked by violence' to a transcendental affirmation of Hope—is as apparent in the play's distinctive technical qualities as in the more direct analytic formulations of its vision that have so far been stressed.

Indeed, to speak of 'analytic formulations' seems a peculiarly fitting procedure in a discussion of this play. For one of its most pervasive, and obtrusive, features is its leaning towards the undramatic on the one hand, and towards the prosaic on the other. Dramatic and poetic immediacy, the vital complexity of an *embodied* vision—a vision rooted in some integral affirmation, and accordingly charged with creative responsiveness to immediate existence—is here either at a discount, or simply beyond possibility of attainment. And so, too, it is not for nothing that this above all tragically weighted play should seek expression in an ostensibly 'comic' framework. For the fullness of tragedy can impinge only in the fullness of a world of 'glory'—a world whose here-and-now are supremely meaningful and precious. As its consummation in the

Cross, the tragedy of the Word *made Flesh*, tragedy can exist, can bring tragic purgation, only in and to a world that is *purgeable*—a world that, when all has been faced, yet remains planted in inexhaustible depths of beauty and worth.

Celia is less than tragic, and so less than triumphant. Tragically triumphant she ought to be, and Reilly does not omit to announce how we are meant to take her. But neither her disillusionment, nor her subsequent martyrdom, remotely touches us as we are touched—well, supremely, by the agony of King Lear and the martyrdom of his Cordelia; or even the glory of Eliot's own Becket. Like the other characters of the play, Celia—the experience that is Celia—is not sufficiently *present* to engage us with even elementary tragic force. She unpacks her heart with words, but there is no degree of 'objective correlative' behind them (and this lack is felt with much greater urgency than it is in *Hamlet*—in the course of whose condemnation, it will be remembered Eliot coined this useful critical phrase). For the largeness of Celia's rhetoric, the 'Four Quartets', as it were, turned into jargon and unsubstantiated gestures—

> For what happened is remembered like a dream
> In which one is exalted by intensity of loving
> In the spirit, a vibration of delight
> Without desire, for desire is fulfilled
> In the delight of loving. A state one does not know
> When awake. . . .

—hardly penetrates our most superficial critical defences.[1] It is not, presumably, suggested that *Hamlet* fails on quite this level. But perhaps (though the distance separating them in achievement remains immense) there may be some causal similarity in the shortcomings of the two works. In *Hamlet*, Eliot suggests, Shakespeare 'attempted to express the inexpressibly horrible'; whilst the tragic materials that lay to his hand were, moreover, peculiarly intolerant to the expression of this recoiling vision. Nihilism, we may generally say, tends to frustrate even its own orderly articulation, and least of all can it find expression in tragic terms. Nihilism is not tragic. It is the antithesis of tragedy—of tragic horror as of tragic glory; it has supped full of horrors (is not Macbeth's tragedy precisely his annihilation within himself of all that makes tragedy possible?): only boredom, and the horror of boredom—

---

[1] This poetic inadequacy would seem to be quite distinct from the author's concern (as described in his Spencer Memorial Lecture, on *Poetry and Drama*) to evolve 'a form of versification and an idiom which would serve all my purposes without recourse to prose, and be capable of unbroken transition between the most intense speech and the most relaxed dialogue' and 'to avoid poetry which would not stand the test of strict dramatic utility'. For whenever the play does approach 'intensity'—as in some of Reilly's speeches and Celia's—the verse tends to be overlaid with a series of stiffly external rootless images, not energized from any vital centre, or to abandon any attempt at imaginative definition, giving way to the vaguest rhetorical inflation.

what you brought with you:
The shadow of desires of desires—

remains. And *The Cocktail Party* presents us with a kind of nihilism; since a nihilistic vision of life remains none the less nihilistic for being pinned to a universe of transcendental affirmation incarcerated in eternity—for ever *beyond* tomorrow's cocktail parties, and tomorrow's drives to Boltwell, and tomorrow's unecstatic nights at home.

And so *The Cocktail Party* is offered not as a tragedy but as 'a comedy' superimposed upon tragic hints and guesses. Such a structure might conceivably serve as a potent means of deepening, and extending, a fundamentally tragic vision. Here, however, one is aware of it mainly as the defensive refinement of a dramtic utterance rarely adequate in dramatization, which thus cannot attain to tragic stature. . . .

From *Essays in Criticism*, Vol. 3, No. 1, 1953, pp. 85–95.

H*

The Confidential Clerk

. . . In *The Confidential Clerk* the grab bag of parents and children on which the plot swings is obviously Eliot's means of dramatizing the larger issue of alienation and kinship among human beings in general. Lucasta comes out with it most explicitly at the beginning of Act II:

> Oh, it's strange, isn't it,
> That as one gets to know a person better
> One finds them in some ways very like oneself,
> In unexpected ways. And then you begin
> To discover differences inside the likeness.   (pp. 61–2.)[1]

Lady Elizabeth, as we come to expect, pierces closer to fundamentals with:

> Of course, there's something in us,
> In all of us, which isn't just heredity,
> But something unique. Something we have been
> From eternity. Something . . . straight from God.
> That means that we are nearer to God than to anyone.   (p. 87.)

In *The Cocktail Party*, Sir Henry Harcourt-Reilly admits his powerlessness to work out the destinies of his patients, thus asserting the power of freedom of the will over deterministic psychology. Here, Lady Elizabeth, touched with the 'Light from the East', recognizes that the course of one's life is not entirely preconditioned by the chromosomes. The two plays are, each in its own way, implicit protests against twentieth-century scientism.

As it happens, the truth of Lady Elizabeth's words 'there's something in us . . . which isn't just heredity', confronts her in a startlingly unexpected way when she learns that the 'worldly and materialistic' Barnabas Kaghan, for whom she has entertained such disdain, is her own son. Moreover, the stern, embittered Mrs Guzzard hardly seems the likeliest of parents for the tenderhearted, gifted Colby. The financial expert, Sir Claude, has fathered a daughter unable to keep track of even her daily expenses. Perhaps that is why Lucasta needs the levelheaded, practical Kaghan, in turn the offspring of a lady who proudly flaunts her contempt for facts and figures. Such incongruities dramatize the theme of free will and the uniqueness of the individual that informs *The*

---

[1] All quotations from *The Confidential Clerk* are from the first American ed. (Harcourt, Brace, New York, 1954).

Confidential Clerk. The burden of what we do or become falls on us, we are led to infer.

'Blood is thicker than water', we often hear. But Eliot brings out in his newest play that blood relationship is not in itself a guarantee of love. Love must be earned and deserved, as is shown by Colby's turning to Eggerson at the end (presumably to replace Eggerson's lost son) instead of to his real parent, as well as Lady Elizabeth's embarrassed overtures to Kaghan and Sir Claude's anguished plea to Lucasta for moral support. There is nothing here of the sentimental mysticism about filial devotion characteristic of some of nineteenth-century fiction (*Bleak House*, for example). With all its artificiality of plotting, *The Confidential Clerk* presents us with a view of parentage and filial obligation that is tough-minded, unflinchingly realistic and unsentimental.

Despite the intimacy of its subject-matter, *The Confidential Clerk* is not simply a domestic drama. It is not about *a* family, but, of course, the entire human family. Indeed, Eliot seems in his latest play to have moved the closest he has come so far to parable and allegory. The flesh-and-blood actuality of most of his characters conceals the fact that they are intended to be representative as well as individual. And unless one is prepared for this dual functioning of the characters, the coincidences and ingenious turns of plot are likely to seem like just so many tricky contrivances. Certain links of the play with Euripides' *Ion*, as well as the echoing of Biblical phraseology throughout its dialogue, obviously tie it up with Western-Christian cultural traditions. But this background serves mainly to counterpoint the basic theme of the play, the threatened disintegration of this culture; and the scrambling and unscrambling of families serves Eliot as a homely means of dramatizing the idea.

One hint of what Eliot is getting at lies in the unprecedented variety of the characters—in the variety, that is to say, of social strata represented. Apart from minor servant characters, *The Family Reunion* and *The Cocktail Party* are each peopled by homogeneous groups, the 'upper crust' in the first play, the upper middle class in the second. *Sweeney Agonistes* is Eliot's single excursion into the opposite end of the social scale. In *The Confidential Clerk* some attempt is made at a vertical cross-section, from Sir Claude and Lady Elizabeth (with the implication that she comes from an even higher-class family than her husband), to Eggerson, the secure, unpretentious middle-class clerk, to the shabbily genteel Mrs Guzzard, to perhaps Eliot's most engaging 'rough diamond', the cockney B. Kaghan, and Lucasta, who with all Sir Claude's attempts to turn her into a 'lady' makes no attempt to conceal her low-life childhood. In this assemblage Colby's part is that of the unwilling parvenu. His background is made purposely vague throughout most of the play, because he is intended as a focal character with points of contact with all the others—loved by Lucasta, admired by Kaghan, related by blood to Mrs Guzzard alone, almost adopted by Sir Claude and Lady Elizabeth, taken over by Eggerson. Not only is there a graduation of social types here, but more of a sense than is usual with Eliot of the interaction of city and country. Sir Claude and Lady Elizabeth are obviously urban; Mrs Guzzard is suburban. B. Kaghan has left the country to make his fortune in the city, whereas Eggerson habitually flees the city where he makes his living for the comfort and quiet of his cottage and patch. Colby again is in between, pulled in both directions. . . .

To be sure, in no play of Eliot's are we made so aware, as we are in *The Confidential Clerk*, of gulfs between people, of incommunicability due not merely to semantic difficulties, but to sheer impenetrability. There is something more than tact and shrewdness in the 'confidences' of Eggerson. He is, especially to Colby, a mystery, enjoying a kind of security the new clerk cannot grasp. 'You know, I think that Eggerson's garden / Is more real than mine', he confides to Lucasta (Act II, p. 64). At the same time, Colby's world is virtually closed to Eggerson, and the other characters can make only groping approaches to it. At a crucial moment in Act II, a social gulf intervenes between Colby and Lucasta, when she mistakes his loyalty to Sir Claude for snobbery. A similar misunderstanding occurs in the concluding scene of the play when Mrs Guzzard, standing on her dignity, is so quick to take umbrage at Lady Elizabeth's rash (though, under the confused circumstances, quite pardonable) questioning of the truth of her testimony. The misunder-standings are 'horizontal' as well as 'vertical'. Sir Claude and Lady Elizabeth have felt cut off from each other during their married life; Lady Elizabeth had felt alienated from her family, just as Sir Claude had from his father, Lucasta from her mother, even Mrs Guzzard from her husband. Lucasta and B. Kaghan, in fact, represent the one natural bond of sympathy in the play ('Nobody could despise *you*, Lucasta; / And we want the same things'; 'B. makes me feel safe. And that's what I want'). One might say that all the characters of the play are 'confidential clerks', in that they all keep secrets not only from each other, but from themselves.

The question, of course, is: Where is the way out of this impasse? And one is found for the people involved here, which may or may not be applicable to all of us. In Sir Claude and Lady Elizabeth, Eliot repre-sents a partial, not total, stage of the cultural disintegration that he has described. It is obvious from the outset that their sensibilities are not 'untrained by either religion or art'. They are both seekers after ultimate reality in their groping ways, though Sir Claude seeks it in a utilitarian sort of art and Lady Elizabeth in a faddish sort of religion. Revealingly, Sir Claude confides to Colby what his pottery means to him:

> I suppose it takes the place of religion:
> Just as my wife's investigations
> Into what she calls the life of the spirit
> Are a kind of substitute for religion.   (Act I, p. 50.)

Sir Claude's perception is partially accurate, but not quite delicate enough. His failure to recognize Lady Elizabeth's genuine spiritual

feeling betrays his own spiritual limitation—'possessed by the craving /
To create, when one is wholly uncreative' (p. 48). His art, appropriately
enough, is artifact, without soul or organism. If his creative activity represents art uninformed by religion, Lady Elizabeth's dabbling conversely represents religion cut off from art—that which gives spiritual
longings concrete embodiment and form. She has, she confesses, desired
all along 'to inspire an artist', as revealed by her early disappointing
marriage to Tony, a poet (apparently a poetaster, as it turns out), and
now her frustrated maternal inclination towards Colby. That makes
doubly pathetic her unawareness of her own husband's artistic leanings.
'I know now that poets don't look like poets: / And financiers, it seems,
don't look like potters', she eventually confides to Sir Claude (Act II,
p. 107). In fact, Sir Claude and Lady Elizabeth, taking the appearance
for the reality, have each accused the other of merely social motives for
marrying. In each others' eyes they represent indeed 'survivors of a
vanishing class', with 'the vestiges of manners', the aspect in which they
appear also to Lucasta and Kaghan. Colby shows himself to be more
effectual as a 'confidential clerk' than Eggerson (for a reason that will
appear later) in bringing their greater potentialities to light.

Kaghan and Lucasta, foundling and bastard, the most rootless people
of the play, are presumably the 'raw stuff' out of which civilization is
made. While on the stage, they may convince us of the joys of the epicu-
rean, materialistic life, but our sober reason persuades us afterwards
that Lucasta of the 'good heart' and Kaghan of the 'shrewd insight'
represent the pre-educated Rousseauistic 'nature' that culture must act
upon. Their different attitudes towards 'civilization' as represented by
Sir Claude and Lady Elizabeth—Lucasta's aggressive mockery of conventional manners, Kaghan's parody of them in his efforts towards
'respectability'—provide, to be sure, some of the most delectable high
comedy of the play. On the other hand, their relationship to Colby
(Lucasta: 'I wish you would teach me how to appreciate [music]';
Kaghan: 'You know, Colby, / You and I ought to be in business together') shows the leavening process of culture taking place.

Much as we commend the union of business and the crafts with the
liberal arts, the joining of 'religious thought and practice' in the persons
of Colby and Eggerson should give us more cause to rejoice. Eggerson,
until Colby happens along, has been the *anima naturaliter Christiana*,
leading a religious life without being able to formulate it. (His gardening
is a natural art, in contrast to Sir Claude's pottery.) Colby, on the other
hand, has a religious bent of mind, but, until he meets Eggerson, he has
no conscious life around which to wrap it. Just as Colby has been unable
to enter Eggerson's garden, Eggerson says 'I wish I was musical' when
he is preparing to introduce Colby to Lady Elizabeth. Their setting out
together for Joshua Park is as happy a pairing as that of Don Quixote
and Sancho Panza, the traditional emblem of imagination combined
with common sense. Colby's choice of the career of church organist
represents the integration of religion and art on its highest level. And

the reuniting of Sir Claude and Lady Elizabeth with their estranged
children—the lowly elevated, the mighty humbled—all alike touched
in some way by Colby and Eggerson, is surely an effective parable of
contemporary society, seeking a unity and an ethos. 'We'd meant to be
married very quietly / In a register office', says Lucasta. 'You must have
a church wedding', affirms Lady Elizabeth. The 'secular' characters are
being brought towards a spiritual state and learning, we may gather, to
aspire to something beyond 'security' and 'respectability'. To quote
from an earlier play:

> What life have you if you have not life together?
> There is no life that is not lived in community,
> And no community not lived in praise of God.[2]

In his concluding long speech, Colby has left his would-be parents, his
real parent, and his adopted parent with his vision of a 'father' common
to them all, who is to be known only 'by report, by documents. . . . By
objects that belonged to him and faded photographs'. Moreover, he has
left them with a conception of the Incarnation that is accessible to
modern mankind. Colby, we realize, is a symbol of the integrating
element so much needed in our contemporary culture. But we are not
yet done with him.

Colby's taking up the career of church organist at the conclusion of
The Confidential Clerk enforces on the mind the pervasive part music
performs throughout the drama. . . . Music is to *The Confidential Clerk*
what poetry is to *The Cocktail Party*. In the more recent play, one can
almost feel music succeeding where words, even at their most eloquent,
fail—in bringing about harmony in human relations. This certainly
seems to be what Eliot intended us to feel. There is a 'peculiar range
of sensibility', he has written, that 'can be expressed by dramatic poetry
at its moments of greatest intensity. At such moments we touch the
border of those feelings which only music can express.' Like Walter
Pater, Eliot looks upon music as the supreme art, the most self-
contained, the perfect fusion of matter and form. At the same time he
recognizes that the poet can only approach the perfection of music,
'because to arrive at the condition of music would be the annihilation of
poetry'. He envisages rather 'a kind of mirage of the perfection of verse
drama, which would be a design of human action and of words, such as
to present at once the two aspects of dramatic and of musical order'.[3]

It is significant, therefore, that Eliot causes his characters in *The
Confidential Clerk* to be stimulated to their highest self-expression
under the influence, direct or indirect, of music. At the end of Act I,
Sir Claude speaks his loftiest thoughts ('I want a world where the form
is the reality. . . .') when he is alone in the presence of Colby, the
musician. Ceramics is his 'music', but it is his fate to be most aware of

[2] Choruses from *The Rock*, II, in *Collected Poems, 1909–1935*, Harcourt,
Brace, New York, 1936, p. 188.
[3] *Poetry and Drama, Selected Essays*, pp. 43–4.

the 'substance' of his art and only dimly to perceive 'form'. He must return from his china to the Potters Association and to 'figures'. Lady Elizabeth too, under the influence of Colby, is moved to her sublimest speech in Act II, where the humbug of 'The Light from the East' is transmuted into a sudden perception of the relation of man to God. It is, in fact, the very sound of the word 'piano' that stirs her to remember at last her relations with Mrs Guzzard. This brings the 'aunt' on the scene eventually to straighten out the tangled relations of the characters. It is unfortunate that after this moment of lucidity Lady Elizabeth must return to her previous state of confusion, but this moment bodes fair for the future. The influence of music is most tangibly represented by Colby's actually playing the piano for Lucasta, presumably the most 'philistine' of the characters. It is at that most luminous moment at the beginning of Act II when Lucasta too reaches the greatest insight into her character and situation, and her greatest feeling of communion with Colby. Ironically, it is after the playing stops, when the two are reduced to the level of words, that their crucial misunderstanding develops. At the end, it is music—through the proffer of the position as church organist—that brings Colby and his spiritual foster parent, Eggerson, together, just as Mrs Guzzard's disdain for her son's inherited profession symbolizes their final separation. One of Colby's roles, after all, is that of the counterpart of Ion, son of the God of the Muses, Apollo, mediator between the divine and human, progenitor of culture.[4] And Mrs Guzzard, in her runic utterance, bears about her the vestiges of the Pythian priestess whose function was to harbour Ion until his identity was to be revealed and he was ready to perform his mission, though in her disillusionment she resembles more the Cumaean Sibyl.

Not only is music an important part of the material of the play, but in its form as well Eliot interestingly seems to be emulating musical structure. In no previous play has he worked so intensively as he does in *The Confidential Clerk* with what he calls elsewhere 'contrapuntal arrangement of subject matter'. Clearly, in *The Cocktail Party* something like the development of the string quartet is aimed at in the juxtaposition of the four lovers, but *The Confidential Clerk* is virtually a *sinfonia concertante* in its modulations and graduations of a simple, unifying theme. The changes rung, the transitions in the mode of treatment of the basic situation of children lost and restored—comic ('bastard'), pathetic ('foundling'), romantic ('changeling'), mystic ('re-incarnation')—recall the movements of the theme-and-variations. Can we not perceive in the constantly shifting relationships of the characters, resolved in a unison at the end, the dramatic counterpart of a fugal development? To be sure, these may seem to be devices at the disposal of the most tone-deaf dramatist, but here Eliot's manipulation of characters in the manner of musical instruments brings to mind his concluding sentence in a recent essay: 'It is in the concert room rather

---

[4] See the beautiful commentary of Hilda Doolittle in her translation of *Passages from Euripides' Ion*, Houghton, Mifflin, Boston; 1937.

than in the opera house, that the germ of a poem may be quickened.' . . .[5]

Undoubtedly there will always be readers or viewers of *The Confidential Clerk* who find the ingenious contrivances and manipulations of the plot jarring and unsuitable to its naturalistic setting. It has already been suggested that these serve a symbolic purpose, that the naturalistic drama is merely a vehicle for Eliot. To a modern audience he cannot present gods controlling human destiny, but through a neatly ordered plot (so absent from contemporary drama that we have grown to regard it as 'artificial') he can suggest that there is some providence that directs our lives. And surely Eliot's causing so many meetings to come off differently than planned, having characters turn up at unexpected times, having so many startling things happen, though in a 'realistic' setting, serves an important cathartic function—to jolt us out of our complacency, to awaken us to a sense of the marvellousness in the everyday life that we are prone to take so much for granted. That is why Eliot's poetry, though it approaches nearer and nearer to the world of music, must remain riveted to colloquial prose.

It is true that Colby Simpkins with all his imposing weight of mythic, symbolic, and naturalistic life remains pretty much of a wraith. The fact is that Eliot still has not succeeded in depicting a saint in *action* in the contemporary world. Just as in *The Cocktail Party* much of Celia's goodness must be taken on faith, we assent to Colby's largeness of soul mainly on the recommendations of others. It is then for what he represents rather than for what he accomplishes that we must accept him. He is the one character of the play who remains a lyric poem. Still, Eliot has moved further than any dramatist of our time in depicting the concrete universal on the stage. Moreover, the very unobtrusiveness with which he fuses the mainstreams of Western drama—the semi-mythic personages of the classical drama, the allegorical representation of the medieval morality, the domestic setting characteristic of the contemporary theatre—probably continues to keep his achievement from being duly recognized.

However, his main claim to the attention of most of his contemporaries is his accomplishment of the goal that he considers most important for the dramatic poet of our time: to incorporate the climate of opinion of his age.[6] By now it is possible to generalize on the 'Eliot-ian' play. With all his subsequent development, he has not departed far from the implications of Lord Henry Monchensey:

The instinct to return to the point of departure
And start again as if nothing had happened,
Isn't that all folly?

[5] '*The Music of Poetry*', *Selected Essays*, p. 465.
[6] 'For the business of a poet is to express the culture in which he lives, and to which he belongs, not to express aspirations towards one which is not yet incarnate' ('The Social Function of Poetry', *Adelphi*, 21, July–Sept. 1945, p. 154). Eliot illustrates with Virgil, Lucretius, and Dante.

His typical plot situation now, as then, is the 'reunion'—a group of individuals, related in some way to each other, separate and then come together again, sobered, sophisticated by an emotional experience they have all shared, presumably better oriented to each other and the world. To a society obsessed with 'adjustment' and 'peace of mind', Lord Henry again suggests an answer, further explored in the later plays:

> I feel quite happy, as if happiness
> Did not consist in getting what one wanted
> Or in getting rid of what can't be got rid of
> But in a different vision.[7]

In *The Confidential Clerk*, of course, this vision is imparted by Colby to all those assembled, in his modern version of the Incarnation:

> I have the idea of a father
> . . . .
> Whose image I could create in my own mind,
> To live with that image. An ordinary man
> Whose life I could in some way perpetuate
> By being the person he would have liked to be,
> And doing the things he had wanted to do. (Act III, p. 147.)

Here Eliot has explored and symbolized with all the resources at his command some of the most perplexing paradoxes confronting twentieth-century man, his loneliness amid the crowd, his incommunicability in an age of communications, his insecurity in an age of prosperity. In his latest play he carried the spoken word to its limits of expressibility, just as he conveys drama far beyond the confines of the proscenium arch. It will be interesting indeed if he can continue 'To go as far in this direction as it is possible to go, without losing that contact with the ordinary everyday world with which drama must come to terms'.[8]

From *PMLA*, Vol. 72, No. 4, 1957, pp. 792–802.

[7] *The Family Reunion*, II, ii. One reason for the relatively static nature of this drama as compared with the later ones is that here we get only the 'after' without the 'before'.

[8] *Poetry and Drama, Selected Essays* p. 44.

PETER MILWARD

The Elder Statesman and *The Waste Land*

... it would seem that in *The Elder Statesman* we are further away from 'The Waste Land' than in any other of Eliot's works. In fact, there is in the whole play only one apparent echo of the earlier poem. But at least it may be worth while to examine this echo, and see if it discloses some deeper significance. In the first act of the play, there is a dialogue between Monica and her father:

> Mon. You know what the doctors said: complete relaxation
> And to think about nothing. Though I know that won't be easy.
> Cla. That is just what I was doing.
> Mon.   Thinking of nothing?
> Cla. Contemplating nothingness.[1]

In these lines it is not perhaps fanciful to detect an echo from the second poem of 'The Waste Land', 'A Game of Chess', which contains a dialogue between a rich lady and her unseen visitor:

>   'Do
> 'You know nothing? Do you see nothing? Do you remember
> 'Nothing?'
>   I remember
> Those are pearls that were his eyes.
> 'Are you alive, or not? Is there nothing in your head?'[2]

True, there is a noticeable difference in tone between these two quotations. In the one case, the conversation is calm and rational, a logical exchange of thought; in the other case, it is wild and frantic, and the answers are as illogical as the questions. Yet there is sufficient similarity in the content of these quotations to justify investigation into the reason for their similarity.

To begin at the end, the passage from *The Elder Statesman* has an importance in the total scheme of the play, in that it serves to introduce us to the fundamental hollowness of Lord Claverton's personality. As a public personage, an 'elder statesman', he leads a life that is empty and meaningless, because it bears no relation to his private self. Indeed,

---

[1] *Collected Plays*, London, 1962, p. 301.
[2] *The Waste Land*, 121–6.

Charles, the fiancé of Monica, has just expressed his doubt as to 'whether there was any private self to preserve'.[3] He is a man who is always playing a part in the eyes of the world, posing as someone he really is not, while all the time he is as it were locked out of his inner, private self; and in consequence, when he is left alone, he has nothing to contemplate within himself. He is what Gomez describes as 'the worst kind of failure'—

> The man who has to keep on pretending to himself
> That he's a success—the man who in the morning
> Has to make up his face before he looks in the mirror.[4]

But now that he is retiring from public life, he has at least become aware of his malady, and this is the first step to his recovery. As he confesses somewhat pathetically to Monica:

> Now, I've not the slightest longing for the life I've left—
> Only fear of the emptiness before me.
> If I had the energy to work myself to death
> How gladly would I face death! But waiting, simply waiting,
> With no desire to act, yet a loathing of inaction.
> A fear of the vacuum, and no desire to fill it.
> It's just like sitting in an empty waiting room
> In a railway station on a branch line,
> After the last train, after all the other passengers
> Have left, and the booking office is closed
> And the porters have gone. What am I waiting for
> In a cold and empty room before an empty grate?
> For no one. For nothing.[5]

If we turn back to 'The Waste Land', we find that this is precisely the situation of modern society as described by Eliot in that poem. . . .

A noticeable feature of 'The Waste Land', both the poem and the reality it portrays, is a certain hollowness and emptiness of the characters presented. They seem to flit in and out of the lines, as ghosts rather than human persons, and it is not difficult for the poet to identify one with the other in his somewhat confusing manner. They all form part of the indistinct crowd he sees walking round in a ring and flowing over London Bridge.[6] So in the second poem, 'A Game of Chess', he begins by presenting a rich lady before her boudoir, but then turns to describe the ornamentation of the room in minute detail, so that the lady herself remains anonymous and impersonal. Next, he shows her

---

[3] *Collected Plays*, p. 300.

[4] Ibid, p. 312.

[5] Ibid, p. 302.

[6] 'The Waste Land', 56, 62. Cf. Note to 218: Characters are said to 'melt' into each other, to be 'not wholly distinct' from each other; 'all the women are one woman, and the two sexes meet in Tiresias'.

in conversation with a partner, who is never introduced, except for the vague 'Footsteps shuffled on the stair'; and the unreality of this partner is emphasized both by her frenzied questions to him and by his strange, inconsequential replies to her. We are made to feel that he is perhaps after all only an effigy stuffed with straw, like Guy Fawkes or Mistah Kurtz—the typical hollow man of the modern age.[7]

This relation between the rich lady and her unseen partner is proposed by the poet as symbolic of the general relation between man and woman in the modern age, a relation that has been degraded by sexual lust from one between human persons to one between mere objects of selfish pleasure. The outcome is a spirit of apathy and boredom, in which human life has lost all joy and meaning, and time is spent 'pressing lidless eyes and waiting for a knock upon the door'.[8] In such an existence, the past survives only in 'a heap of broken images'[9] the present is fugitive and uninteresting, and the future remains vague and menacing:

But at my back in a cold blast I hear
The rattle of the bones, and chuckle spread from ear to ear.[10]

The movement of this hollow age is inevitably towards the hollowness of the grinning skeleton in 'death's dream kingdom'.

Here is a real social problem, which the poet has set out to describe in poignant terms in his poem, and for which he seeks a remedy—but in vain. The conditions for the return of fertility to the 'waste land'— Give, Sympathize, Control—which he proposes in the concluding poem, remain unfulfilled; and he leaves us with a glimpse of the lone figure of the Fisher King (himself):

I sat upon the shore
Fishing, with the arid plains behind me
Shall I at least set my lands in order?[11]

In the midst of a hollow and selfish age, he feels like a man imprisoned in the tower of self, 'le Prince d'Aquitaine à la tour abolie',[12] unable to enter into fruitful contact with other human persons.

A similar criticism of modern society as hollow and empty recurs in 'Four Quartets', notably in the third stanzas of 'Burnt Norton' and 'East Coker'. In 'Burnt Norton' Eliot describes the contemporary world as 'a place of disaffection' under a dim light, which is neither the day-

---

[7] 'The Hollow Men' has two epigraphs: one from Conrad's novel, 'Mistah Kurtz—he dead'; the other, the traditional cry of small boys going from door to door on Guy Fawkes Day (5 Nov.), 'A penny for the Old Guy'.

[8] 'The Waste Land', 138.

[9] Ibid., 22.

[10] Ibid., 185–6.

[11] Ibid., 400–2, 423–5.

[12] Ibid., 429, a quotation from a sonnet of Gerard de Nerval, included here because of its association with the 'horrible tower' of Ugolino (Dante's *Inferno*, XXXIII, 46) referred to in 411–16.

light of joy in God's creatures, nor yet the darkness which purifies the soul with deprivation:

> Only a flicker
> Over the strained time-ridden faces
> Distracted from distraction by distraction
> Filled with fancies and empty of meaning
> Tumid apathy with no concentration
> Men and bits of paper, whirled by the cold wind
> That blows before and after time.[13]

The ultimate fate of these men, who are faces rather than human persons, is described in 'East Coker' (with echoes of Milton's 'Samson Agonistes'):

> O dark dark dark. They all go into the dark,
> The vacant interstellar spaces, the vacant into the vacant,
> The captains, merchant bankers, eminent men of letters,
> The generous patrons of art, the statesmen and the rulers,
> Distinguished civil servants, chairmen of many committees,
> Industrial lords and petty contractors, all go into the dark,
> And dark the Sun and Moon, and the Almanach de Gotha
> And the Stock Exchange Gazette, the Directory of Directors,
> And cold the sense and lost the motive of action.[14]

Here we come upon a further point of contact with *The Elder Statesman* in the explicit mention of 'the statesmen and the rulers' among those who are going into the dark; like Lord Claverton, they too are described as vacant and lacking in motive for action.

In the particular case of Lord Claverton, the general movement 'into the dark' is characterized as a flight from the past, his own past self. He himself states this explicitly.:

> What I want to escape from
> Is myself, is the past.[15]

But at the same time he fully recognizes that

> Those who flee from their past will always lose the race.[16]

He has attempted to do so by the trivial expedient of changing his name and his former connections, only to find that he is followed by the ghosts of his past, in the material shape of Gomez and Mrs Carghill, who have likewise changed their names in the meantime. These ghosts perform the providential function of forcing the man, however painfully, to face himself; and it is when he at length decides to do so,

[13] 'Burnt Norton', 90–105.
[14] 'East Coker', 101–9. Cf. Milton, 'Samson Agonistes', 80–9.
[15] *Collected Plays*, p. 337.
[16] Ibid., p. 333.

that his inner problem is solved. But this is no easy decision to make, and when it is made, the credit belongs not to the ghosts, who are presented as simply malignant beings, but to Monica's love for her father. It is to her that he makes his confession, and in her that he at last finds himself; and this, as he declares to her, is 'the first step taken towards my freedom.'[17] The outcome is for him a deep, interior peace of soul,

> It is the peace that ensues upon contrition
> When contrition ensues upon knowledge of the truth.[18]

or as Charles observes soon after:

> He's a very different man from the man he used to be.
> It's as if he had passed through some door unseen by us.[19]

Thus in his final play Eliot presents us with his solution to the problem of 'The Waste Land'. It is, in effect, remarkably similar to that of Shakespeare's final plays, which have always exercised a deep influence on his work. On the one hand, the early poetry of Eliot contains significant echoes of *Antony and Cleopatra* and *Coriolanus*; and the particular quotation from 'A Game of Chess' discussed above contains echoes of *Hamlet* (III, iv—Hamlet and his mother) and *King Lear* (I, i—Lear and Cordelia),[20] as well as a direct quotation from *The Tempest* (I, ii—Ariel's song). On the other hand, his final play reflects the fundamental theme of growth in self-knowledge in *King Lear*. By heeding the empty flattery of his wicked daughters and handing over the reality of his kingdom to them, the old king comes to realize how hollow is the mere title, without the corresponding power, of a king.[21] Through bitter experience of his daughters' ingratitude he learns to recognize himself as 'a poor, infirm, weak and despised old man' in the midst of the storm; but the fullness of his self-recognition comes when he wakes from his sleep of madness in the arms of his true daughter, Cordelia, and in his realization of her love he realizes how he has deserved his sufferings.[22] Similarly Eliot's solution in *The Elder*

---

[17] Ibid., p. 344.
[18] Ibid., p. 353.
[19] Ibid., p. 354.
[20] *Hamlet* III, iv, 131–3: Q: 'To whom do you speak this?' H: 'Do you see nothing there?' Q: 'Nothing at all, yet all that is I see.' H: 'Nor did you nothing hear?' Q: 'No, nothing but ourselves.' *King Lear* I, i, 88–92: L: 'Speak.' C: 'Nothing, my lord.' L: 'Nothing!' C: 'Nothing.' L: 'Nothing will come of nothing. Speak again.' Cf. also Conrad: *Heart of Darkness*, p. 31: 'Do you see him? Do you see the story? Do you see anything?'
[21] *King Lear* I, iv, 143–6: F: 'Can you make no use of nothing, nuncle?' L: 'Why no, boy, nothing can be made out of nothing.' F: 'Prithee tell him so much the rent of his land comes to;' also 162–4: L: 'Dost thou call me fool, boy?' F: 'All thy other titles thou hast given away. That thou wast born with.'
[22] Ibid. III, ii, 20, and IV, vii.

Statesman consists simply in Lord Claverton's recognition of himself, which is brought about by the filial love of Monica ('This love is silent'); and the play ends with the ideal marriage of Charles and Monica, like that of Ferdinand and Miranda in *The Tempest*. Thus in 'the certainty of love unchanging'[23] modern man, here represented by Lord Claverton, learns to unlock the door in his heart and to enter that 'Garden where all loves end'[24], where he finds himself at rest in 'the still point of the turning world'[25].

... Modern man is imprisoned in himself, as it were in a 'horrible tower'; and after initially shrinking from the 'overwhelming question', like Prufrock, he is soon forced to ask the critical question whether there is any possibility of escape. This is the question of 'The Waste Land', which is also borne in on the mind of Lord Claverton; and the answer turns out to be in the nature of a paradox: the way out of the prison of self is both exit out of oneself and entrance into one's inner self in the movement of love. It is this love, whether between parents and children, or between husband and wife, or between friends, which reveals man's true self, not merely as one individual distinct from every other, but as intimately united with another on a personal basis. This is what makes Charles exclaim in his love for Monica at the end of the play:

So that now we are conscious of a new person
Who is you and me together.

And Monica replies, by pointing to a yet higher love:

I've loved you from the beginning of the world.
Before you and I were born, the love was always there
That brought us together.[26]

Moreover, in this same love ... Eliot establishes a vital connection between the end of the play and the beginning of 'The Waste Land'. For love is the meaning of the spring rain, that pierces the drought of March and stirs the dull roots in the dead land, 'mixing memory and desire'[27] and drawing past and future together in an eternal present when

All shall be well and
All manner of thing shall be well
When the tongues of flame are infolded

[23] *Collected Plays*, p. 334 and p. 335.
[24] 'Ash Wednesday' II.
[25] 'Burnt Norton', 62, 136. Cf. D. Maxwell: *The Poetry of T. S. Eliot*, London, 1952, p. 156: 'The still point evidently suggests the stillness of eternity, and contrasts with the fevered movements of the temporal.'
[26] *Collected Plays*, p. 355.
[27] 'The Waste Land', 1–4.

Into the crowned knot of fire
And the fire and the rose are one.[28]

From *Studies in English Literature* (Tokyo), English number, 1967,
pp. 4–13.

[28] 'Little Gidding', 255–9. Cf. H. Gardner, *The Art of T. S. Eliot*, London,
1949, p. 183: All shall be well, when all is gathered in love, and the rose, the
symbol of natural beauty and natural love, is one with the fire, the love by which
all things are made. "Little Gidding" is a poem of fire, the fire which is torment
to the self-loving, purgation to the penitent, and ecstasy to the blessed, and it
closes with mortal and immortal life united in the resurrection symbol of the rose
of heaven'; and p. 184: 'The subject of each poem and of the whole poem ("Four
Quartets") is Christ, Alpha and Omega, the Beginning and the End, Author and
Finisher of our Faith.'

Select Bibliography

SOME EDITIONS OF THE WORK OF T. S. ELIOT

The Complete Poems and Plays of T. S. Eliot, Faber and Faber, 1969.
Collected Poems 1909–1962, Faber and Faber, 1963, re-issue 1965.
Collected Plays, Faber and Faber, 1962.
Selected Poems, Faber and Faber, 1962.
Selected Poems, Penguin Books, 1948.
The Waste Land: a Facsimile Transcript, Faber and Faber, 1971.
The Four Quartets, Faber and Faber, 1944.
The Sacred Wood, Methuen 1920, 2nd ed. 1928 (University Paperbacks 1960).
For Lancelot Andrewes, Faber and Faber, 1928 (revised as *Essays Ancient and Modern*, 1936).
The Use of Poetry and the Use of Criticism, Faber and Faber, 1933.
Points of View, Faber and Faber, 1941.
On Poetry and Poets, Faber and Faber, 1957, re-issue 1969.
Selected Essays, Faber and Faber, 1932, 3rd ed. 1951, re-issue 1958.
Selected Prose, Penguin Books, 1953.

CRITICISM

F. W. Bateson, 'T. S. Eliot: the Poetry of Pseudo-Learning', *Journal of General Education*, 1968, Vol. 20, No. 1.
Staffan Bergsten, *Time and Eternity: a study in the structure and symbolism of the* 'Four Quartets', Heinemann, 1960.
C. A. Bodelsen, *T. S. Eliot's Four Quartets*, Rosenhilde and Baggen (Copenhagen), 1958.
M. C. Bradbrook, *T. S. Eliot*, Longmans, Green, 1950.
David Daiches, 'T. S. Eliot', *Yale Review*, Spring 1949.
Donald Davie, 'The Dry Salvages', *Twentieth Century*, Vol. 159, No. 950, 1956.
Johannes Fabricius, *The Unconscious and Mr Eliot*, Nyt Nordisk Forlag, Copenhagen, 1967.
Helen Gardner, *The Art of T. S. Eliot*, Cresset Press, 1949, re-issue 1968.
Helen Gardner, *T. S. Eliot and the English Poetic Tradition*, Nottingham University, 1966 (pamphlet).
D. E. Jones, *The Plays of T. S. Eliot*, Routledge and Kegan Paul, 1960.
Genesius Jones, *Approach to the Purpose*, Hodder and Stoughton, 1964.
Hugh Kenner (ed.), *T. S. Eliot: a Collection of Critical Essays*, Prentice Hall Inc., 1962.
Hugh Kenner, *The Invisible Poet: T. S. Eliot*, W. H. Allen, 1960.
C. G. Martin (ed.), *Eliot in Perspective: a Symposium*, Macmillan, 1970.
F. O. Matthiessen, *The Achievement of T. S. Eliot*, Oxford University Press, 1935, enlarged edition, 1947.
Orbis Litterarum (Copenhagen), Vol. 14, No. 1, 1959 (contains several good articles on Eliot).

T. S. Pearce, *T. S. Eliot*, Evans Bros, 1967.

Raymond Preston, *The* 'Four Quartets' *Rehearsed*, Sheed and Ward, 1946.

R. H. Robbins, 'The T. S. Eliot Myth', *Science and Society*, Vol. 14, No. 1, 1949-50.

Kristian Smidt, *Poetry and Belief in the work of T. S. Eliot*, Jacob Dybward (Oslo), 1949.

Allen Tate (ed.), *T. S. Eliot : the man and his work*, Delacorte, New York, 1966.

Leonard Unger (ed.), *T. S. Eliot : a selected critique*, Rinehart, New York, 1948.

Leonard Unger, 'Images of Awareness', *The Sewanee Review*, Vol. 74, No. 1, 1966.

Margaret C. Weirick, 'Myth and Water Symbolism in T. S. Eliot's *Waste Land*', *Texas Quarterly*, Vol. 10, No. 1, 1967.

Raymond Williams, 'T. S. Eliot on Culture', *Essays in Criticism*, Vol. 6, 1956.

George Williamson, *A Reader's Guide to T. S. Eliot*, Thames and Hudson, 1955, 2nd ed. 1966.

Yfor Winters, *Anatomy of Nonsense*, New Directions, Norfolk, Conn., 1943.